KANT

KARL JASPERS

KANT

EDITED BY HANNAH ARENDT

TRANSLATED BY RALPH MANHEIM

A HARVEST/HBJ BOOK

A Helen and Kurt Wolff Book

HARCOURT BRACE JOVANOVICH

NEW YORK AND LONDON

DE

Originally published in German as part of
Die grossen Philosophen I
by R. Piper & Co. Verlag, München, 1957

Acknowledgments

Acknowledgment is made for permission to use the following: For the quotations from Kant: *Critique of Aesthetic Judgment,* trans. by John Henry Bernard (Hafner Library of Classics Series), New York, Hafner Publishing Company; *Critique of Practical Reason,* trans. by Lewis White Beck, University of Chicago Press, copyright 1949 by the University of Chicago; *Critique of Pure Reason,* trans. by Norman Kemp Smith, Macmillan & Company Ltd. and St. Martin's Press, Inc.

CONTENTS

KANT

I. LIFE AND WORKS

1. *Life*

Immanuel Kant (1724–1804) was the fourth child of a Königsberg saddler. Some of his ancestors had come to Germany from Scotland. He was raised in an atmosphere of Pietistic Christianity. Later, as tutor in the family of Count Keyserling, Kant often "thought with emotion of the incomparably finer training he had enjoyed in his own home, where he had never heard or seen anything wrong or immoral." Beginning in 1740, he studied philosophy, mathematics, and theology at Königsberg. From 1747 to 1755, compelled by his father's death to earn his own living, he served as tutor in various families. At the end of this period he was appointed lecturer at the university, which meant living on his lecture fees. He twice applied in vain for a professorship in philosophy at Königsberg; in 1764 he declined a chair in poetry at Königsberg and offers from Erlangen and Jena. Finally, in 1770, he was appointed professor of logic and metaphysics at Königsberg. In 1778 he declined an appointment at Halle, which, like the previous calls, would have brought him considerably larger earnings. In 1796 he gave up his lectures for reasons of old age. In 1798 his health began to decline and in 1804 he died in a state of senile dementia.

Kant was unusually small, thin, flat-chested; his right shoulder was higher than his left. He was frail but fundamentally healthy. Hamann called him the "little schoolmaster." In the decade he spent working on the *Critique of Pure Reason,* he often spoke of his health. All his life he suffered from complaints of various sorts and was always worrying about his diet. It was from 1781 to 1791, when he was putting his other great works into final form, that he spoke least of his health.

2. *Kant's World*

In Kant's time, Königsberg was a lively commercial center, a city open to the world. Aristocrats and merchants, academicians and men of letters met freely. The Russian occupation from 1758 to 1762 introduced a new ease into social relations. In those years Kant, the artisan's son, lost his awkward-ness and grew to be an accomplished gentleman. Hamann tells us that he was carried away by a whirl of social distractions. Among his friendships, that with Hamann was noteworthy. Although they were far apart in their modes of thought and religious views, there was never an actual breach between them. "In comparison with Kant's," Hamann wrote, "my poor head is a broken jug, clay beside iron." But he continued forthwith: "All this chatter about reason is pure wind; speech is its organon and criterion" (Hamann in a letter to Herder VI, 365). And when Hamann tried to ex-plain to him Herder's *Alteste Urkunde des Menschengeschlechts,* Kant, for his part, requested: "but if possible in the language of human beings. For I, poor son of earth, am not organized to understand the divine language of contemplative reason" (Letter 78).

Kant remained a bachelor. On two occasions he seemed to be on the way to marriage. But he hesitated so long that the ladies turned elsewhere. Later, he said: "When I needed a wife, I could not support one."

Kant kept no household, but lived alone with a manservant. When not invited out, he took his meals at hotels, always with a group of friends. It was only at the age of sixty-three that he engaged a cook and set up house-keeping. There were always guests at the midday meal. It was now that his daily program, from five in the morning until ten at night, took on the regularity characteristic of the familiar portrait: the elderly professor by whose movements his neighbors set their watches.

Kant was attached by affection and habit to his Königsberg surroundings. He could never make up his mind to accept any of the brilliant offers made him by other universities. In declining, he asked indulgence for his "tempera-ment that cannot resolve to make changes which seem trifling to other men" (Letter 44). Kant never even took a trip worthy of the name. Only once in his life did he venture somewhat beyond the borders of East Prussia. He owed his wide knowledge of the world to his constant reading and his imagination. In conversation with a visiting Englishman, Kant spoke so vividly of St. Peter's that the other was convinced he had been to Rome.

3. *Kant's Intellectual Development*

Despite poverty and great practical difficulties, Kant was dominated from the very start by his thirst for knowledge. Asked by a professor why he was studying theology, Kant replied: From love of knowledge. Later, as a pro-fessor, he advised his students to do as he had done, to take an interest in all the sciences, even those of which they did not intend to make a career. At the age of twenty-two, he published his first work, *Ideas Concerning the True Estimation of Living Forces,* dealing with a problem drawn from the intellectual world of Descartes, Newton, and Leibniz. It tells us how Kant foresaw the course of his life. "There is," he writes, "a good deal of presumption in the words I am about to pronounce: the truth, for which the greatest masters of human knowledge strove in vain, has for the first time presented itself to my understanding. I should not dare to justify such a thought, but neither did I wish to renounce it. . . . If one is in a position to persuade oneself that one can catch a Herr von Leibniz in errors, one does everything in one's power to make one's supposition come true. . . . Here is my starting point. I have marked out the path I mean to follow. I shall start on my way and nothing will prevent me from continuing." Never again did Kant take this tone.

Kant forwent all adventures, uncertainties, distractions; he never made any attempt to modify his perspectives by so much as a change of scene. To be sure, we see the intense concentration of a thinking which persistently transcends itself, which penetrates to unsuspected depths—an effort almost unparalleled in the history of philosophy, for it was accomplished without the creative energy of sudden inspiration, without crises and reversals. Thus, though Kant's life is a life of knowledge, it is also far more. He grounded his existence in an unswerving humanity.

"I myself," he wrote circa 1762, "am by inclination a seeker after knowledge; I thirst for it and well know the eager restlessness of the desire to know more and the satisfaction that comes with every step forward. There was a time when I thought all this was equivalent to the honor of humanity, and I despised the common herd who know nothing. Rousseau set me right." The "blind sense of superiority is vanishing. I am learning to honor men and should regard myself as far more useless than a common workingman did I not believe that this occupation [philosophizing] might lend value to all others and help them to establish the rights of humanity."

Kant frequently expresses this attitude, both in his writings and in personal remarks. As late as 1797 he wrote, on the occasion of a literary controversy: "For what can all our labors and all our speculative quarrels avail us if they detract from the kindness of our hearts?" In his senile old age, Kant rose as his doctor entered the room and, when the physician protested, declared: "Humanity has not forsaken me to that point."

4. Kant's Lectures

Kant was a professor. He lectured fourteen to twenty-two hours a week. The subjects ranged from mathematics and physics to logic and metaphysics and further included physical geography, anthropology, pedagogy, and natural theology. Kant never lectured on his own philosophy. As was customary at the time, he expounded the works of other authors, though sometimes he remarked: What the author says here is wrong. His lectures, as we can see from those that have been published, were far more traditional and dogmatic than his written works. He wished to communicate knowledge, to teach his students how to think for themselves, to reinforce their ethical feeling. Herder, who heard him lecture in the sixties, tells us that he "had the joyful vigor of a youth. His broad forehead, built for thinking, was imperturbably serene. To hear him teaching was to enjoy the most delightful company. No object of knowledge was indifferent to him. He returned over and over again to the unbiased knowledge of nature and to the ethical value of man. He compelled one to think independently, despotism was foreign to his nature."

5. Particular Events

There are no decisive turning points in Kant's life. His conflict with the Wöllner ministry over his lectures on the philosophy of religion (1794) has become famous. He was accused, in a harsh statement by the cabinet, of having degraded and distorted the fundamental doctrines of Holy Scripture and Christianity. Kant justified himself but accepted the injunction to cease lecturing on the philosophy of religion. He allowed his freedom as a teacher to be curtailed. He did not become a martyr but, like Spinoza, acted circumspectly. In 1766 he had written to Moses Mendelssohn: "Although there are many things that I think with the clearest conviction and utmost satisfaction but shall never have the courage to say, I shall never say anything that I do not think." Kant's life was built on a need for peace and security. He was never morally at odds with himself. Who would dare to ask for more!

6. The Works

The chronology of Kant's works is as follows:

After his first work published at the age of twenty-two (1746), there was an interruption of eight years. From then on, one work followed another except for the period from 1770 to 1781, when he published next to nothing. Though naturally a prolific writer, he was now virtually silent. For it was in those years that what we know as the Kantian philosophy developed. The work which established it once and for all, the *Critique of Pure Reason,* was published in 1781. A clear dividing line is drawn between the "critical" and "pre-critical" works. Beginning in 1781 (Kant was then fifty-seven), the following works were completed in rapid sequence: *Prolegomena to All Future Metaphysics* (1783), *Idea for a Universal History with Cosmopolitan Intent* (1784), *Foundations of the Metaphysics of Ethics* (1785), *Critique of Practical Reason* (1788), *Critique of Judgment* (1790), *Religion Within the Limits of Mere Reason* (1793). And in between, a number of important shorter treatises appeared. Kant himself attached so much importance to the distinction between the pre-critical and critical works that he regarded the early work as devoid of interest. "Through this treatise [*Critique of Pure Reason*] the value of my earlier metaphysical works was totally destroyed." When a new edition of his complete works was projected, he wished it to begin with *On the Form and Principles of the Sensible and Intelligible World* (1770), which, though not yet an embodiment of the critical philosophy, represents an important step toward it.

It is an impressive picture. Kant was already a celebrated philosopher and brilliant author when, in his mature years, he arrived at the basic ideas to which he owes his historical importance. If he had died at the age of fifty, we should have no Kantian philosophy. He would only be for us a noteworthy figure of the Enlightenment, comparable to Garve or Mendelssohn. Undeterred by any considerations of vanity, he devoted more than ten years to the painstaking elaboration of his ideas. His compelling preoccupation was to make use of the short remaining years to give the world the irreplaceable thoughts that had come to him. This modest man knew that a world of ideas had been born in his mind, which he alone could communicate. His haste made him indifferent to form. Full of his task, consumed by his idea, Kant knew ten years of amazing productivity after his ten years of silence. It was then that he organized his life to the point of pedantry. If he had not strictly husbanded his forces, the achievement of his old age would not have been possible.

Kant's posthumous works include many notes and manuscripts. Kant had not said his last word. He continued to work until his mind failed and even afterward. His fundamental idea led him to ever new perspectives. Even in the last notations, the Kantian spirit is sometimes present, though it is clear that his mind is declining: the thought breaks off, his memory fails, he has lost his free command of language, he clings obstinately to certain set ideas and is no longer receptive to the new. His advancing illness led to an un-Kantian perversity. His belief that he had found his way to a definitive truth is understandable and necessary. What is not necessary is that, at variance with statements he himself had made not so very long before, this belief should have taken the form of an insistence on the literal truth of his writings and an inability to suffer contradiction in conversation.

The *pre-critical* works reflect the scientific interests, human attitudes, experience of the world, questions in logic and metaphysics, which provided the background of his later, critical thinking. A first group of the precritical works dealt with natural science. These include the celebrated *General History of Nature and Theory of the Heavens*. Kant was first to conceive the theory that the Milky Way was a vast agglomeration of suns related in kind to the remote elliptical nebulae, one of which, Andromeda, can be seen with the naked eye. Other treatises deal with the rotation of the earth, earthquakes, fire, the winds. Natural science remained one of the foundations of the later critical philosophy.

A second sphere of his interests consisted in geography and anthropology. Beginning in 1757 he lectured on physical geography and in 1772 inaugurated a course in anthropology. He expressed the opinion that "one of our students' main failings is that they learn too soon to juggle with reason, lacking sufficient historical knowledge to replace experience of their own." In these lectures Kant wished to communicate knowledge "of man as a citizen of the world." To this end, he collected an abundance of geographical, historical, and general facts based on the knowledge of men he had obtained by "association with his fellow townsmen and compatriots," on wide reading of travel books, history, biographies, and even of "plays and novels." This wide field of knowledge provided the substance of some of his pre-critical works, such as his *Observations on the Sense of the Beautiful and the Sublime*. Critical philosophy brought new light to his interpretation of this material. It is here that Kant's works on politics and the philosophy of history have their roots. This too is the source of many observations and examples in his ethical and religious works. In his old age, he published some of these lectures under the title *Anthropology from a Pragmatic Standpoint*. His interest in man, as in other matters, was vastly deepened by the critical philosophy. But to the end he could write such sentences as: "Philosophy is in reality nothing other than a practical knowledge of men." The fundamental question of philosophy, encompassing all others, remained for him: "What is man?"

A third sphere of interests, the realm of logic and metaphysics, was with him from the first. As early as 1755 Kant wrote on the first principles of metaphysical knowledge. Beginning in 1762, he published a number of important papers on logic. Thence the way led directly to critical philosophy.

The achievements and interests disclosed in the pre-critical works do not yet, properly speaking, add up to the Kantian philosophy. But they did make him one of the most brilliant philosophers of the Enlightenment. He is characterized as a man of the Enlightenment by his cultivated literary language, which he later abandoned in favor of a penetrating, dense, sober, technical style. His fine serenity and irony, his unfanatical openness to ideas and facts, the keenness and flexibility of his thinking which at once set about questioning its own products, his inclination toward experience in every realm of the world, and the skepticism that accompanied his undying love for metaphysics—all these made him a man of the Enlightenment.

II. KANT'S ROAD TO CRITICAL PHILOSOPHY

1. *The Pre-Critical Writings*

A. We consider Kant's pre-critical writings in order to observe the movements of thought that helped to create the state of mind in which the critical philosophy could be born.

In his student years Kant became acquainted with traditional ontology and metaphysics through theological categories and the philosophy of Wolff and Leibniz. He shared their fundamental certainty, their questions and problems. But in his dealings with his predecessors and contemporaries he strove for one thing above all: indubitable certainty.

In his habilitation thesis, *New Light on the First Principles of Metaphysical Knowledge* (1755), in which he refers to Crusius, his first question is: How far does the power of logic extend? Kant thinks: there is nothing without a determining cause. We think the existence of God as a being who exists with absolute necessity, because the opposite, the thought that nothing whatever is, is unthinkable. But this impossibility of the opposite is only the cause of our knowledge of His existence, not the ground of His existence itself. "He exists; to say this is to have said and understood everything concerning Him."

This train of thought distinguishes the ground of being (or becoming) from the cause of knowledge. The former is the determining, productive ground which determines a priori, the latter is the cause that determines a posteriori, that merely explains. If we think that God or absolute, unconditional being necessarily exists because the opposite is unthinkable, what is lacking in this line of reasoning is the a priori determining ground of the existence of an absolutely necessary being.

Thus there is no proof of the existence of God. Possibility and impossibility provide no basis for apprehending the existential ground. "Possibility" means that two connected concepts do not contradict one another. Concepts result from comparison. But if nothing is given, there is no room for comparison. Hence nothing can be represented as possible except for what in every possible concept is real and has existence, and indeed, in the last analysis, absolutely necessary existence. If we denied this, nothing whatever would be possible, there would only be the impossible. If God is done away with, not only is the whole existence of things destroyed, but their inner possibility as well. "Of all beings, God is the only one in whom existence comes first, or is identical with possibility. And no concept of His possible existence remains if we deny His existence."

In these ideas, Kant strives to penetrate to what precedes every possible thinkable. Being and thinking are not the same. Thinking presupposes reality. Reality may not be taken as logical necessity. The logical necessity of what we must think is not the real necessity of being. *Logical relations may not be mistaken for real relations.* Being cannot be derived and constructed from logical necessity.

The same point, that logical and real relations must not be confused, is argued in his article "An Attempt to Introduce the Concept of Negative Quantities into Philosophy" (1763): Contradiction in thinking (logical opposition) is something fundamentally different from the reality of conflicting forces (physical antagonism). To conceive of a body which is at once moved and not moved is a contradiction. But a body that is simultaneously impelled in two opposite directions by two equal forces is not in a state of contradiction, but in a state of rest. In logical contradiction thought negates itself; what is thought in this way is no-thing. The contradiction of opposing forces is possible as the reality of rest. A logical negation has no reality. Real opposites, however, can be combined: pleasure and pain, love and hate. Analyses of concepts throw light only on logical contradiction, not on the real opposition of forces.

B. After the question of how far the power of logic extends came the question as to the origin of certainty. Kant shared the passionate desire of his scientific era for reliable knowledge. Mathematics was the ideal. Since the seventeenth century, philosophers had taken it as their guide. Many of them were great mathematicians. It was with Kant that a change set in. For him too (although he was not an inventive mathematician and probably not even in possession of higher mathematics) mathematics retained its uncontested rank. To his mind, a science was a true science only insofar as mathematics was contained in it. But he questioned the *scope* of mathematics and thus inquired into the *difference between philosophical and mathematical knowledge.*

In mathematics the fundamental definitions are synthetic, that is, they are explained by a perceptible operation. In metaphysics the fundamental definitions are analytic, that is, they are tautologies, in which the intended meaning is merely clarified.

Mathematics combines given concepts of clear and definite quantities in order to see what can be deduced from them. In metaphysics concepts are articulated which are given in a state of confusion. In mathematics my concept of objects arises through explanation. In philosophy I have no clear concept of a thing but must first look for such a concept. Mathematics makes use of signs, metaphysics of words. In metaphysical thinking, accordingly, one must always have the reality itself in mind. Metaphysics cannot exchange the representation of things for the clearer and more convenient representation of signs, but can consider only universals in the abstract. The signs of mathematics are concrete instruments of knowledge that we can use with the certainty of having left nothing out of consideration. Words, on the other hand, merely help us to recollect universal concepts, whose meaning one must always keep directly in mind.

It is more difficult to analyze complex insights (in philosophy) than to combine simple data by synthesis and so draw conclusions (in mathematics). Consequently, "metaphysics is the most difficult of all human disciplines; but a metaphysics has never yet been written."

Kant recognizes the unique importance of mathematics but frees philosophy from its tutelage. Though at that time Kant did not yet distinguish between the modes of certainty prevailing in mathematics and in philosophy—in both he found indemonstrable axioms and demonstrable inferences—he saw a difference in modes of indemonstrability, which provided the foundation of his ultimate insight. From this difference it follows that mathematics and philosophy have different tasks, different methods, and different kinds of certainty. Mathematics is rejected as a model to be imitated; but mathematics remains a basis of orientation insofar as the autonomy of philosophy is brought out by a comparison with mathematics.

Kant agrees with Crusius that, in addition to the axiom of contradiction, there must be another foundation of knowledge, namely, indemonstrable and self-evident principles, the first material principles of human reason. But he rejects Crusius' proposition that "What I cannot think otherwise than as true, is true," insofar as this proposition purports to express a ground of truth. For what it says is precisely that no ground of truth can be indicated and that knowledge is therefore indemonstrable. "A sense of conviction is an avowal, not a compelling argument."

c. We perceive the extent of Kant's doubt. After distinguishing between the logical and the real (and so demonstrating the inadequacy of mere thinking) and after ascertaining that philosophy, as opposed to mathematics, must seek a certainty of its own, Kant did not directly set out to build this new philosophy. His next step was, rather, *to doubt the possibility of any metaphysics.* His fine clarity became, for the present, a clarity of nonknowledge. He was too honest, too intent on certainty to evade the issue. In the *Dreams of a Visionary Explained by the Dreams of Metaphysics* (1766), he takes a critical view of his own thinking and ridicules ideas that he himself had pursued. Taking Swedenborg's delusions as an example, he shows what a wide variety of things are conceivable, and he goes on jokingly to formulate such conceptions in order to show that as such they are mere fantasies. Metaphysical hypotheses, he declares, are so flexible that they can be fitted to every fairy tale. Men build "various kinds of intellectual castles in the air," and each inhabits his own, that is, he dreams. For that, as the Greek saying (Heraclitus) has it, is the difference between dream and waking: in dreams each man has his own world, while in the waking state we all have one world in common. He draws a parallel between Swedenborg's delusion and that of the metaphysicians. And as to supernatural vision: "Knowledge of the other world can be achieved here below only at the cost of some portion of the understanding we need for this world."

The work on visionaries was an accounting, not an expression of despair. It showed that Kant was prepared to think along new lines. But the new thought was not yet in his possession.

2. *The Turning Point*

The turning point can be situated roughly in 1766. The Kantian philosophy was born in the years from 1766 to 1781 (when the *Critique of Pure Reason* appeared). It was then that he published virtually nothing. In 1770, on the occasion of his appointment to the professorship, he published the required dissertation. It contains a first step (the doctrine of the subjectivity of the intuition of space and time), but not yet the new philosophy.

The sixties and early seventies were the period of his urbane philosophizing, his participation in social life, his detached ironic restlessness, his merciless criticism of his love for metaphysics, the period of great flexibility and rapidly changing perspectives. It is as though Kant had flung himself into a whirlpool of thought and experiences in which he kept finding principles by which to order and articulate his ideas only to throw them away in favor of new insights without as yet being able to put his feet on firm ground.

In the eyes of his contemporaries, Kant was at the height of his career, in possession of the full sovereignty of his intellect, the most elegant and impressive philosophical writer of the time. He mastered the world of dogmatic thought, but rather than submit to it at any point, he corroded it with his skeptical reflection. No one suspected that all this was a prelude.

A. We have a number of noteworthy statements by Kant about his attitude in those years:

He tells us that he had not established himself at any point in the philosophy of pure reason and had written no great books about it; thus, in defending it, he had not been compelled to maintain any one opinion. In the little essays that he scattered about to avoid seeming wholly idle, he had still been playing. But "merely from the state of mind that I put myself into and steadily preserved" and "from the length of time during which I kept my mind open to every new inspiration," he had expected more gratifying results for his philosophizing than any of his predecessors had achieved.

B. By themselves, openness, skepticism, and patience led nowhere. If Kant's negative insight was not to be mere resignation, he would have to find new certainty along new paths of metaphysical thinking.

Kant took a decisive step by introducing method into his skepticism. "I tried quite seriously to prove propositions and their opposite, not in order to demonstrate a theory of doubt, but because I suspected an illusion of the understanding and wished to find out where it resided. The year '69 brought me great light." Kant discovered the antinomies—the world is finite, the world is infinite; it has a beginning in time, it has no beginning in time; everything happens in accordance with causal necessity; there is freedom at the beginning of the chain of causality; and he discovered that the antinomies make their appearance when we seek the whole, when we look for the absolute in the world, or, to put it differently, when we try to make a finite object of the infinite. Here, as he immediately realized, he found a firm methodological basis. "Approximately a year ago," he wrote in September 1770, "I arrived at a concept which I believe I shall never have to change, though no doubt it will require amplification. Through it all sorts of metaphysical questions can be appraised according to perfectly certain and simple criteria, and through it one can determine with certainty whether or not they are susceptible of solution."

c. Another step brought clarity concerning space and time; it was set forth in his dissertation, *On the Form and Principles of the Sensible and Intelligible World*. For Newton space was something absolute, real in itself, the *sensorium dei*. For Leibniz space was the manifestation of the spaceless reality of the monads and their relations. Because space as such does not exist, Leibniz denied the infinite divisibility of space, the reality of empty space, and the possibility of action upon distant objects (all this in opposition to Newton). Kant now professed (with Leibniz) the phenomenality of space, not however (contrary to Leibniz) as unclear appearance, but as the clarity of the sensible world. And Kant professed the objective reality of space (again contrary to Leibniz) as the pure form of our sensible reality, as the condition of the reality of phenomena. As early as 1758, Kant recognized, with Leibniz, the relativity of space (*New Conception of Motion and Rest*). In 1768 (*On the First Cause of the Difference of Objects in Space*), on the basis of a study of the symmetrical phenomena of right and left, image and mirror image, he recognized its objective reality as a form of intuition. There are, between bodies, differences that are purely spatial and not conceptual in nature. The world of space and time is not reality as such, but neither is it illusion; space and time are the conditions of the objective reality of all our sense experience, given in intuition.

This put a new light on the immemorial difference between the natural world given to the senses and the supernatural that transcends sense perception. For Kant the old ontology was still in force: the forms of thought apply to being itself. But now he had confined mathematics to its proper realm, where it was dominant: mathematics comprehends the necessary forms of all sensory intuition. As late as 1770, Kant still held that the concepts attained to intrinsic being. As the forms of sensory intuition apply to the world, so the concepts apply to the intelligibles. Knowledge retains its access to the natural world as well as to the supernatural. Hence the difference between the *mundus sensibilis* and the *mundus intelligibilis*.

From the outset Kant accepted as self-evident the ill-defined traditional view that thinking is the adequate source of knowledge. But what is thinking? Where does it find its ultimate ground? What is the source of the concepts? These questions spurred him on.

In his prize essay, *Principles of Natural Theology and Ethics* (1763), Kant looked upon the "indissoluble concepts" as the foundation of knowledge. But what are they? The fact that the ground through which we know God's being is not the ground through which He is—or in more general terms, that the ground of cognition is not the ground of reality—has consequences for ontology. For example, it is not through logic that I know causality. Rather, causality contains something unfathomed that is present in the "indissoluble concepts." At that time Kant seems on certain occasions to have equated indissoluble concepts with the concepts of experience, which mere logical thinking must await but cannot produce, and, on other occasions, to have held that they complete the concepts of experience, thus enabling us to think originally not only about what can be experienced by the senses but about the supersensible as well.

Simultaneously with this work, Lambert's *New Organon* appeared. He was on the same path, and the two men exchanged ideas. Their desire for certainty led them to inquire into the origin of concepts. They agreed that concepts are forms by which to express relations, that they have their function only in the elaboration of contents of experience. Both opposed Leibniz. In substance, they were already in opposition to the later constructive idealists who looked on the indissoluble concepts as the consciousness of the intellectual function as such and believed that they could obtain knowledge of reality through constructive operations of the mind, without verification in experience.

Kant already felt himself to be on his definitive way (to Lambert, December 31, 1765) and expressed "some confidence" in the insight he had acquired. "Before true philosophy can arise, it is necessary that the old philosophy destroy itself." But this crisis gave him "high hopes that the long-desired great revolution in the sciences is not far off." Of himself he says: "After so many upsets in which I have always sought the source of error or insight in the nature of the method followed, I have finally come to the point where I regard my method as secure."

The correspondence between Kant and Lambert broke off, because Kant felt that he was on the threshold of new discoveries and hesitated to speak before achieving clarity concerning them. Only then would he write and submit them to Lambert for his criticism. Kant now arrived at a totally new method of investigating and deriving the indissoluble concepts, while Lambert merely sought to derive their basic forms from language.

Kant and Lambert both held that the function of thought was to elaborate the concepts of experience, to provide knowledge of reality. But for Kant this was only the beginning of the problem. He inquired, *first:* How is it possible, through the concepts of thought, to gain access to something wholly different, the sensible world? And *second:* How is it possible that concepts which we produce should relate and apply to being as such?

These questions were still based on the standpoint of the dissertation (1770): Space and time do not exist as such, but are forms of intuition.

Sensory perceptions merely represent things as they appear; the intellectual concepts, however, represent them as they are. Kant's conclusion (which was not new) was of great importance for the purification of the traditional ontology, which however still remained in force: when we think of what being is as such, we must not transfer to it any element of sensory intuition, space and time. "When something is conceived not as an object of the senses, but, through a universal and pure concept of reason, as a thing or substance, extremely false positions emerge if we try to subject the thing or substance to the fundamental concepts of sense perception." "The most universal laws of sense perception play, though they should not, a certain role in metaphysics where it is only concepts and principles of pure reason that count" (to Lambert, September 2, 1770).

This much was clear. Everything seemed to be in order. We can and must know reality through the empirical concepts of spatiotemporal intuition, and know the supersensible through pure concepts. But on this foundation, the never-resting Kant conceived the more comprehensive and fundamental question which was ultimately to overturn the presuppositions of all previous thinking.

3. The New Question

The new question, in its simplest form, was this: "On what foundation rests the relation to the object of what is termed our representations?" (Feb. 21, 1772). The answers he attempted to give to this question led Kant to an entirely new path, on which the limits, not only of sensory perception but of thinking itself, would become apparent. The old ontology, the thinking in concepts believed to apply directly to the world of objects, would have to be abandoned. It would become clear that not only the concepts of sensory intuition, but concepts of every kind, are inadequate to the apprehension of being as such. Yet both intuition and concepts have objective significance. The question is: What kind of object do they relate to? And at the same time the question once more arises: We intuit in space and time and we think in concepts; what is the source of the agreement between the object and the representations provided by intuition or concepts?

Various answers are conceivable: The representation of the object is the manner in which the subject (passive) is affected by it; the representation is the manner in which the thinking subject (active) produces the object. "But neither is our understanding with its representations the cause of the object (except for the good purposes in ethics), nor is the object the cause of the representations of the understanding (in sensu reali). The pure concepts of the understanding must, to be sure, have their source in the nature of the mind, but this does not mean that they are brought about by the object or that they produce the object."

Here Kant discerned an extraordinary riddle, a riddle which all of us live with and ignore and which men have lived with and ignored for thousands of years. The thing that I know is not myself; what is it then? I am not unless I have objects, sensory data, before me; what indeed am I without them? I have no outside vantage point from which to compare the subject and object of thought. All I can compare is objects and a subjectivity turned object.

With Kant the new question had taken this form, which was to prove highly effective. How is agreement between representation and reality possible? Or more precisely: How is agreement possible between our intellectual representations, which are based on inner activity, and objects we have not produced by our inner activity?

Kant finds the agreement quite understandable in mathematics. For here the objects before us become quantities only because we can produce their representation by repeating the number one as often as necessary. But it is quite another matter where qualities are concerned. We think causality, substances, and other categories. We think principles such as: Nothing happens without a cause; the quantity of matter is neither increased nor diminished. How is it possible that we should form concepts of things, with which the things necessarily agree, that we should devise principles to which experience conforms, when our concepts and principles do not spring from experience? "This question always leaves behind it an obscurity in regard to our faculty of understanding: whence does it derive this conformity with things themselves?"

Kant questions other philosophers. Plato traces knowledge back to a previous intellectual intuition of the world of Ideas. Malebranche interprets knowledge as the perpetual intuition of the primal essence, as a seeing of things in God. Crusius (following Leibniz) held that God implanted in us rules which harmonize with things and serve as a basis for judgments and concepts. This *deux ex machina* strikes Kant as the most absurd of all answers to the question. None of these solutions convinced him.

The question itself must be formulated more radically. This is the new element in Kantian thinking. He gives the problem new depth by making a question of what had hitherto been regarded as self-evident: the existence of the relation between subject and object. The thinkers cited by Kant, and all thinkers before him, had clung to the standpoint of our natural consciousness, namely, that in matters both immanent and transcendent, in our knowledge both of the world and of God, we confront objects which are real; that we see, hear, think, and recognize them; that we are oriented intentionally toward them; that, like them, we are real—and that this state of affairs represents an ultimate limit that our thinking cannot surpass. Philosophers had indeed inquired concerning the agreement between thought and object, but they had not investigated the possibility of a relation between the thinker and the object; they had not asked what the thinker and the object are and precisely what agrees with what.

The natural attitude has been called "naïve realism." Whether earlier thinkers held the empirical view that we know everything by experience, or the rationalist view that we apprehend the fundamental truth of things by thinking alone, they shared the belief that in cognition the subject confronts an object which he knows. As to the reason for the agreement, the empiricist answer was: Because the things themselves enter into us through our sense organs, and leave their copy or imprint. However, not all sensations are "real," but only those which communicate the force, extension, and resistance of matter. Since Democritus, primary and secondary sensory qualities have been distinguished. But once such a distinction was introduced, all qualities became questionable. This answer led ultimately to a questioning of the reality of the outside world and to a complete skepticism in regard to the knowledge of reality.

The rationalist answer was: There must be agreement because the mind itself produces knowledge, and because what is necessarily thought is real. But in response to the question of how the mind's product, whose necessity is still no proof of the reality of its content, nevertheless conforms to this reality, there was no help but to invoke pre-established harmony: God disposed things in such a way that what we necessarily think always agrees with being as such.

Kant left all these questions and answers behind him by inquiring into the subject-object relationship itself. The presupposition of all previous thinking, the fixed, enduring, unsurpassable relation between subject and object, which as such had not become an object of questioning, because no one had achieved awareness of it as such, now became a question. Kant declared that the subject-object relationship is not the absolute being that precedes all else; that it comes not first but second. And thereby he laid open an area of infinite possibilities. Kant seems to have recognized at once that he was doing something absolutely new. "I noted that something essential was still lacking [i.e., in the dissertation], something which, indeed, [is] the key to the whole secret of metaphysics."

The question of subject and object has been answered by the mystics of virtually all epochs. They transcended the subject-object relationship through the experience in which it was suspended. Their language is full of profound references to what is neither subject nor object but transcends them both. But such experience was made possible only by changes in the state of consciousness, causing both I and object to vanish. The transcending of subject and object implied a mystical union of opposites.

Plotinus taught that existence in the subject-object relationship is not absolute, but a second thing: the One is indivisibly one, more than thought, transcending it. The second thing is the intelligible, supersensory realm of thought in the dichotomy between thought and its object and between one object of thought and another. But in Plotinus this is a mere construction of the supersensory. For him the solution of the problem is in ecstasy.

In India, too, the riddle is considered, but only to be solved by the meditation that rises to higher states of consciousness.

In Kant we have something very different. He remained within our natural state of consciousness, characterized by the dichotomy between subject and object. Living in this state but wishing to think beyond it in order to understand it, he was, as we shall see, compelled at every step to face a seemingly but not really insuperable difficulty. Taking the subject-object dichotomy as his standpoint, he was obliged to speak objectively of that which is the condition of all objectivity. By speaking in objective forms of the condition of all objectivity, he drew what was supposed to transcend the dichotomy into it. The seeming contradiction that this introduces into his whole philosophy is actually a tension which is an intrinsic part of it and must in turn be examined. Kant was seldom aware of it. He ignored it. He did not methodically investigate the method that he followed in practice.

But if we succeed in illuminating the fundamental relation of our subjectivity to objects in such a way as to become truly aware of the special nature of the Encompassing in which we are, then, in examining our consciousness, that is, our thinking, we shall become aware, not only of its limits but also of the presence of the Other. The question becomes possible: How can this Other show itself indirectly in consciousness which is identical with the subject-object dichotomy? To this question Kant gave the richest answers. To be sure, he makes it clear that we live as though imprisoned in the subject-object dichotomy, in space and time and our forms of thought, but he shows how at the same time consciousness frees us from our prison.

Kant's answer to the question of the ground of our cognition will be: We know things in the world, because we have produced them, not in respect to their existence (for in their existence they must be given), but in respect to their form. Thus our concepts are valid only in the realm of possible experience. Outside it they are empty because without objective meaning. They can have objective meaning only in experience, in reality based on sense perception.

But this answer is only an element in a great, comprehensive new philosophy, which, indeed, it first made possible, but which is so far from being exhausted by it that in relation to the total content of the philosophy this element ceases to be anything other than an indispensable methodological instrument.

Now we shall turn to the work. After our characterization of Kant's path from pre-critical to critical thinking, the steps in which are symptoms, not the substance, of the philosophy that was taking form, we must now consider the complete edifice. First of all we shall have to acquire the indispensable insight, gained by Kant, into our cognitive faculty as a whole.

III. STRUCTURES OF KANT'S THEORY

OF KNOWLEDGE

Kant's ideas can be outlined in different ways. All such outlines have been attempts to simplify and clarify. It is hard to see what room there is for further outlines. Yet Kant's thinking is a matrix of seemingly inexhaustible possibilities, and I too shall now venture a résumé attempting to distill his meaning from his actual words. Our first topic will be what is known as Kant's "theory of knowledge."

In our résumé, ideas and proofs are set forth as Kant stated them. In considering them, we must keep in mind what we have just learned about the fundamental direction of Kant's thinking. We do not mean to weary the reader by referring back to it at every step and reminding him of the restrictions and reservations it entails. But it must not be forgotten that what is clearly definable in the thinking we are about to expound is misleading unless we become increasingly aware of an indefinable undercurrent.

1. *The Dichotomy*

Consciousness operates in the dichotomy between the thinking subject and the thought object. In cognition, I judge spontaneously, but not in the void. For if my acts of thought have objective bearing, it is because they are filled with intuition of something that is given to me, toward which I am receptive. Consequently, there are two components of knowledge to be discussed, spontaneity and receptivity, or understanding and sensibility.

2. *Sensibility, Space, and Time*

Whenever I know something through intuition, something is given me. Kant calls this "sensibility." "Intuition is never anything but sensuous." What I as a physical subject encounter in space affects my sense organs. This physiological reality is for Kant only a metaphoric expression (and at the same time a particular instance) of being as being-given. Sensibility covers everything that intuitively fills the act of thought, sense perception in the more restricted usage, the self-perception of the "inner sense," the obscure being of what is thought but not elaborated in thinking.

Without sensibility there is no reality. Regardless of whether, as in physical investigations, it is measurements that provide the criterion of reality, or perceptible documents and monuments as in matters of history, or physiognomic expression as in psychological questions—in every case it is a factor that must be added, something that is made present by an act of intuition. From the standpoint of method, sensibility may perform very different functions in the cognitive process. But in every case it is our witness to reality.

Sensibility is not the system of sensation, which is merely a physiological-psychological abstraction by which we investigate sense perception. Sensibility in the Kantian sense is physical actuality as such, which, to be sure, can never be without sensation. There is an erroneous tendency to take the forms of sensibility in too narrow a sense because Kant, in setting forth the nature of cognition, takes only exact science as his guide. He does not explicitly go into the other varieties of empirical investigation.

Let us consider an object: this table. It is immediately given in intuition. I have sensation of color, light, and shade. If I deduct everything pertaining to sensation, I still have extension and form, or spatiality. This space is intuitive but not sensory in the manner of sensation (sensations pertain to particular sense organs; space does not). But this table before my eyes is more than sensation and space. First, there is its objectivity as such; the table exists for me only through an act of confrontation in which sensation and space become an element of the object. Further, this object has the character of substance (in its force of resistance). Thus we have three factors: the material of sensation; space as a form of intuition; and the category of substance. They are not co-ordinated, but one within the other, the later encompassing the earlier. With such considerations, we are not analyzing the table. Rather, we are taking it as an example in order to inquire what in a real object is present to knowledge. An analysis of the table would disclose its being composed of real parts; analysis of objective reality as such discloses three elements of an undivided whole: sensation, spatiotemporal intuition, category. If from the idea of the table we remove everything that the understanding thinks with its concepts, and everything that pertains to sensation, there remains a pure intuition as the mere form of appearance: space. Time can be separated out in the same way. Space and time prove to be unique pure forms; nevertheless they are not concepts but intuitions.

The first question that now arises is: Are space and time reality as such, which exists even without subjects that know them, hence absolute reality? Or are they forms of intuition that spring from the subject, which through them forms objects and without which objects cannot exist for it? Is their reality contingent on the subject? Kant took the latter view, which he demonstrated in two ways.

First, his "argument" on space makes clear its unique nature: (a) Space cannot be withdrawn from experience because it is, from the very start, at the base of every experience. What I perceive as real, I perceive in space. It is the condition of the existence of any object for me. (b) Space is a necessary a priori intuition. It is impossible to form a representation without space; but one can conceive of a space without objects. (c) Divisions of space do not precede space as the components of which it is put together;

they are encompassed in it. Divisions of space are not specimens of the generic concept *space,* but parts which the one space contains within it.

Secondly, this "argument" is followed by a "proof": In geometry we know a priori—not by mere concepts, but in the medium of intuition—relationships which turn out to apply to reality. The insights of geometry are not gained from experience but are verified in experience. How is this to be accounted for? The subject, by its form of intuition, recognizes a reality that has previously been formed by it.

The conclusion is: Space cannot be an attribute of a thing in itself, but only of things insofar as they are present for a subject, that is, insofar as they are phenomena. And if we removed all the particular conditions of intuition, no space would remain. Because we can consider the particular conditions of sensibility as conditions, not of the possibility of things as such, but only of their manifestation, we may say that real things can occur for us only in space.

When things as such appear to us in space, this does not mean that they do not necessarily do so for all possible subjects. "For concerning the intuitions of other thinking beings we cannot judge whether they are bound to the same conditions that restrict our intuitions." Only "from the standpoint of man," can one speak of space.

In connection with time, Kant adduces similar arguments and proofs. There is only *one* difference. Space is the form of our intuition only of outward things, while time is the form also of the inner sense, and hence of all phenomena whatsoever. Time itself, in keeping with its all-embracing character, cannot be outwardly intuited. Our representation of it takes spatial form; for example, we draw a line.

This view of space and time as forms of our intuition of things and not as realities in themselves is called idealism. Idealism existed before Kant. There were philosophers who conceived the world as unreal or who questioned the reality of the outside world. To Kant this question was a "scandal of philosophy." He says: The world is appearance, not illusion. In other words, space and time have reality, objective validity in respect to all outward objects that can come our way, and inner validity in respect to our inner subjectivity. They have ideality because the things that appear to us are not things in themselves. Kant expresses his idea briefly as follows: Space and time have empiric reality, but transcendental ideality. The thing in itself can never appear to us.

It is clear from Kant's opposition to the philosophy of Leibniz and Wolff that he recognized the autonomous reality of the sensible world existing in space and time. Leibniz and Wolff regarded sensory knowledge as a confused, indistinct knowledge of the understanding. Kant saw that the difference between sensibility and thinking has nothing to do with degree of distinctness. There is distinct sensory intuition and indistinct thought, and conversely. The worlds of sense and thought are not distinguished by degree of distinctiveness but by a fundamental diversity of origin.

Today Kant's views are subject to criticism. We differ from Kant in distinguishing: *first,* the intuition of space, subject to psychological investigation; *second,* the objective space of physics; and *third,* mathematical space. Kant knew nothing of the non-Euclidean space that cannot be represented. He did not yet distinguish directly intuited psychological space, which is by no means Euclidean, from the Euclidean, three-dimensional space that we intuit indirectly. Despite its a priori development, Euclidean geometry applies only to the relatively restricted space of our earthly world, not to that of the cosmos.

It has been supposed that this refutes Kant. Such a refutation, however, does not apply to his philosophical idea of the phenomenality of sensuous existence in space and time, but only to his particular formulations. For everything we know as reality must enter into some mathematical forms that can be known a priori. It is true that the wealth of these forms and the modes of reality have today been explored to a degree that Kant and his age could scarcely surmise.

3. *Thinking*

Matter given to the senses, space, and time was the one factor in our knowledge; the other was thought. In opposition to all previous philosophy and to his own view as late as 1770, Kant came to the conclusion that not only space and time but all forms of our thinking enable us to see things as they appear, not as they intrinsically are. Why? Just as we first acquire an ordered sensibility through the subjective forms of intuition, space and time, so we produce the forms of the things of experience by the subjective forms of our thinking, the categories. It is not only in space and time but also in the forms of thought that we frame, as it were, everything that exists for us.

What we thus perceive has phenomenal reality, but it is not reality "as such." Just as there is "no world as such" that is spatial and temporal, so also there is no "being as such" that is thought and thinkable. Every object of thought is produced by us in respect to its form. It is no longer tenable to distinguish between the *mundus sensibilis* as what gives us the appearance in space and time and the *mundus intelligibilis* as what gives us being as such.

But something that does not exist in itself can, because it is produced in respect to its form (though not in respect to its existence) by the subject with its forms of intuition and thought, be known as an empirical reality.

A. In substantiation of this insight Kant employs the distinction between *analytic and synthetic judgments,* which serves him as a key with which to penetrate the essence of cognition. Analytic judgments only make clear what we already know in a concept as such. For example, in the judgment

"All bodies have extension" the concept of the body already contains extension, as it does form and impermeability. This is an analytic judgment because it clarifies and analyzes our knowledge but does not increase it. Synthetic judgments, on the other hand, are those in which the predicate adds something new which cannot be gleaned from the concept itself. For example: "Some bodies are heavy" is, according to Kant, a synthetic empirical judgment, for the concept of the body as such does not include heaviness. This difference between analytic and synthetic judgments, or between judgments which clarify and those that amplify, is obviously not a distinction according to formal logic (such as affirmative and negative judgments), but one based on the significance of judgments for knowledge.

The evidence of analytic judgments is based on the principles of identity and contradiction. What is the source of the evidence of synthetic judgments? By what indications do we recognize that a predicate not already implicit in the concept of a subject attaches to that subject?

Analytic judgments are present in thinking apart from experience, where we discern nothing new and merely clarify things that were known unclearly. Synthetic judgments, on the other hand, are present in all our empirical knowledge. By perception and observation we find out what belongs together, what follows what. These are judgments after experience (a posteriori), not preceding it (a priori). Synthetic a posteriori judgments are empirical judgments.

B. But are there also *synthetic judgments a priori?* Kant answers: Yes, in mathematics and the natural sciences. In his view, all mathematical judgments are synthetic (e.g., $7 + 5 = 12$; a straight line is the shortest distance between two points), for the result does not follow analytically from mere concepts, but is guided by intuition or enumeration, that is, based synthetically on construction in space and time of the mathematical a priori concept. According to Kant, synthetic judgments also occur in the natural sciences; for example: All changes have a cause.

Such principles in science are necessary and universally valid judgments. Without them no sure knowledge would be attainable. No statement would be true except in regard to past experience; in other words, the validity of all statements would be only relative. Compelling scientific knowledge is possible only thanks to the validity of such principles as the principle of causality and the law of the conservation of matter. Otherwise, things would appear and disappear accidentally, events would take place without a cause, there would be miracles. There would be no more knowledge but only fairy tales. But this is not the case. The more science advances, the more evident it becomes that natural laws govern all happening that is accessible to knowledge. The presupposition of science is demonstrated by the findings of science.

Thus, according to Kant, there are synthetic a priori judgments in science;

they are its principles (and such questions as whether these synthetic judgments a priori can be definitively formulated, whether they are adequately described by such laws as the principle of causality or the law of the conservation of matter, whether their formulations change with the progress of knowledge, are without crucial bearing on the fundamental philosophical idea).

But if there are synthetic judgments a priori that are not, like mathematical judgments, acquired through the a priori intuition of space, and not, like empirical judgments, acquired a posteriori through sensory intuition, how then are they formed? Where is the ground of their truth? In thinking itself, insofar as it does not operate only with the concepts of formal logic (analytically) but also produces objects in respect to the form of their intelligibility. In mathematics thought was able to build on the a priori intuition of space. Thinking can conceive of itself as the productive function, and as such it can apprehend all the a priori conditions of objectivity, which are the categories of all intelligibility.

c. With this the broad horizon of thought is opened. Within it lies everything that exists for us, even perception. The example of the table before us shows that thought contains the matter of sensation, the form of spatial intuition, the category of substance. Thus *understanding is present in every perception.* Thought is not merely something that is added afterward; it is already present as categorial form in every objective intention. The understanding is at work in the structure of every object we come across. In perceiving substance, we think causally. Perception in itself is a thinking. The chaos of sensation, the mere unconscious stimuli and reactions of an organism conceived as an object of biology, precedes thought and does not, itself, think. If we do not live in a chaos of sensations, if we do not drown in unconscious stimuli and reactions, but instead see form, order, relationships, it is because the categories have given form to the chaos. It is because the understanding with its categories first builds up the empirical world, that it can later gain knowledge of it by conscious investigation.

d. Thus far we have been speaking of thought, which produces the form of everything we can know. Everything that exists for us is an object of thought. It is thought which transforms sensory intuition into perception and cognition. What I cannot touch, even remotely, in objective thinking, what I cannot in some way "know," does not exist for me. The question of being becomes the question of being-thought.

The nature of thinking became a question for Kant at an early date. In 1762 he stated that all thought is judgment. What then is "the secret force through which judgment becomes possible"? "At present I incline to believe that this force or capacity is nothing other than the power of the inner sense, i.e., its ability to make its own representations the object of its thoughts. This faculty cannot be derived from something else, it is fundamental." But this was only the beginning. The idea that thought is judgment was to be stated by Kant over and over again, in well-nigh infinite modifications, yet with a remarkable unity of direction. We shall try to sum up Kant's thinking in this matter.

(1) "Thinking is the act of relating a given intuition to an object." There is no object that is not cogitated; and there is no thinking without an object. Mere intuition would be an objectless jumble of sensations. Only when an act of thought intervenes is there an object.

(2) The existence of an object presupposes differentiation. An object is this object (identity) only insofar as it is not another. But at the same time every object is in itself "one and other"; the thought of it presupposes a subject and predicate. Thus thought is a perpetual separating and combining.

(3) An object has unity in thought only by virtue of a unity of action. To think is "to combine representations in one consciousness." "Judgments are functions of the unity of our representations."

(4) All thinking includes the "I think" that "must be able to accompany all representations." This I, which is identical with itself, corresponds to the unity of the judgment and its object. All thinking moves within this unity. To depart from it is to fall into confusion, distraction, chaos.

It is objective unity that gives thought its validity. Objective unity is grounded in the supreme subjective unity that Kant terms "transcendental apperception." "Judgment is the method of raising cognitive data to the objective unity of apperception."

This basic function is also called "synthesis." Synthesis produces thought in respect to its form. The concept is the result of such synthesis. Thus Kant rejected the notion that concepts arise through the abstracting of the universal from many cases. In his view, what is universal in a thought content is the product of concrete synthesis.

(5) Only sensory intuition relates immediately to the object. It is always isolated. When the intuition becomes an object, something universal, the category, enters into it. Thus no cogitated object is grasped in its immediacy; it is always mediated. If I expressly think of an object, I differentiate and define it, that is, I think it through the concept. Objectivity as such is the most universal category under which particulars can be subsumed. Or, as Kant sums up: "Since no representation other than direct intuition reaches the object, a concept never relates directly to the object but always to some representation of it (whether intuition or already a concept)."

All this is summed up in this thesis: The understanding is discursive, not intuitive. It passes back and forth between separate things that it combines; by way of mediation it arrives at the immediate; it knows through concepts which are never the object itself.

4. *Derivation of the Categories from Judgments*

Kant terms such basic forms of thought as substance and causality the constitutive categories because they produce the forms of empirical objects in the world. If the object is not something alien to thought, but is, in respect to its form, produced by thought, category and form of judgment will indicate one another. They have a common origin in the "I think" of transcendental apperception. If thought constitutes objects, the fundamental forms of judgment must provide a guide by which to find the fundamental forms of the categories. What constitutes unity in the judgment must also constitute the unity of the object. Thus Kant derives the categories from the different kinds of judgment. From the general principle of thought, as implied in the system of the forms of judgment, he seeks to determine the ultimate conditions of intelligibility, and from these to derive the categories which constitute all reality, the forms of everything that can occur in the world for us.

In the *Critique of Pure Reason,* the forms of judgment (quantitative: universal, particular, individual; qualitative: affirmative, negative, infinite; relational: categoric, hypothetic, disjunctive; modal: problematic, assertoric, apodictic) are presupposed as given. The categories are now derived from the forms of judgment in such a way as to make evident the abrupt passage from a relation expressed intellectually in a judgment to a constitutive relation between objective realities. To the categoric judgment "A is B" corresponds the categorial relation of substance and accident; to the hypothetic judgment (if A is, B is) corresponds the relation of cause and effect, and so on. The categories, according to Kant, are as follows. Quantitative: unity, multiplicity, universality; qualitative: reality, negation, limitation; relational: substance, causality, reciprocity; modal: possibility, impossibility, existence, nonexistence, necessity, contingency.

Kant was convinced of the completeness of his tables and judgments. They underlie the system of all his great works. Despite certain artificialities, they proved wonderfully fruitful and remain an object of our respect. But the fundamental idea must be distinguished from the way in which it was elaborated. The twelve forms of judgment and the table of twelve categories derived from them met with the approval of few of Kant's followers. The system has parallels in other systems of categories which, particularly after Kant's time, were exceedingly widespread (the most significant being that of Hegel's logic). None of them succeeded in its purpose of producing a universally binding conception of the totality and structure of our basic categories.

But though Kant's tables were by no means definitive, there is a crucial and enduring element in his basic idea. Kant held that, though we do not experience the categories, we become aware of them in connection with experience. Thus it is permissible to think that new experience may enrich and clarify the system, though without ever making it final. In fact, there is no theoretical reason why in the course of time new categories should not be discovered ad infinitum. But then Kant's claim to definitive completeness must be abandoned.

5. *The Two Stems*

One fundamental idea recurs again and again: our knowledge springs from two stems, sensibility and understanding. By the former objects are given, by the latter they are cogitated. In the subject receptivity is coupled with spontaneity. The a posteriori is linked with the a priori, perception with function. In each case we have the same relation. Kant speaks of two sources, two origins, the birthplace and the germ of knowledge.

The two sources are interdependent. It is their unity that first gives rise to knowledge. The fundamental cleavage of subject and object signifies that only subject and object together make knowledge possible. Consciousness is always passive and receptive; but it is an act of thought that makes the affection into an object. Consciousness always thinks, intuitive sensibility first gives the act of thought objective significance.

Sensibility as such is inarticulate, infinite, meaningless. Not conceived as an object and hence not cogitated, it remains an aimless jumble. It is mere existence, which does not yet stand before me, the indeterminate which, with all the fullness of its immediacy, is as nothing. It is a reality which, being undefined, is not yet a reality. At the same time understanding which only thinks, to which nothing is given, is incapable of cognition. We are dependent on sensibility.

Understanding requires intuition if it is to become cognition rather than mere thought. Intuition requires understanding if it is not to remain a mere subjective jumble, if it is to become an object and thus take on objective meaning. In short: "Thoughts without content are empty, intuitions without concepts are blind."

Both intuition and understanding have an intrinsic a priori factor. Intuition is not only receptive sensibility but has the a priori forms of space and time, just as the understanding has the a priori forms of the categories.

Kant calls this a priori factor, taken by itself, "pure," while he terms the content that gives objects their existence "empirical." Thus space and time are pure, while color, audibility, tangibility are empirical. The categories, for example, substance, causality, are pure, while real things and particular causal relations, bodies and movements, are empirical.

In Kantian thinking there is a twofold dichotomy, or we may speak of two overlapping dichotomies: The opposition between the subject (the spontaneity of thinking) and the object (the receptivity of sensibility) reappears within the object itself as that between form and matter. The subject-object dichotomy is on the one hand inseparable from objectivity and on the other hand lies in the structure of the object itself. The object is built from the matter of intuition and determined by the form of the category. Matter and form correspond to object and subject, for the matter is given while the form is cogitated. We can analyze the object itself according to matter and form without thinking of its relation to the subject through which alone its object-character is possible. That is the link between the two oppositions which cut across one another: form exists through the spontaneity of the subject's thinking; matter exists through the receptivity of the subject's sensibility. Thus we have, on the one hand, subject, form, a priori, pure, and, on the other hand, object, matter, a posteriori, empirical.

This Kantian thinking is often said to be dualistic. Mistakenly so. Kant says that perhaps the "two stems," sensibility and understanding, "spring from a common root which is unknown to us." But here a limit is reached; the common root can no longer be derived. Kant speaks of the "secret of the origin of our sensibility." "This peculiarity of our understanding, that it can produce a priori unity of apperception solely by means of the categories, and only by such and so many, is as little capable of further explanation as why we have just these and no other functions of judgment, or why space and time are the only forms of our possible intuition." The mystery of the origin recurs in a new form when he speaks of the imagination which mediates between the understanding and sensibility and makes the former applicable to the latter; it is, says Kant, "an art so deeply hidden in the human soul that we shall hardly ever pierce the veil with which nature conceals its actual operations and attain a clear view of them."

What does it mean when Kant expressly and repeatedly says that the common root of our cognition, of the two stems, is a mystery? He does not derive the dichotomy of subject and object from a conceptual One as the source of all things, but explains how being becomes actuality for us in this dichotomy and how, through the elucidation of the area in which we think, we can perhaps, in our thinking, pass beyond it, transcend it.

In the elucidation of the medium in which we live and think, Kant is dualistic. But the two sources of knowledge are not to his mind two principles of being; rather, being is invoked as the one root, which remains unknown to us. Being is conceived dualistically only in respect to the form through which we gain awareness of it. Kant's metaphysics is not dualistic in the sense of conceiving two primal powers, such as God and matter. He does not give us a "dualistic *Weltanschauung*." But he is impelled to think dualistically for the purpose of exploring a field in which paths to unity are subsequently sought and found.

6. Not Being but Consciousness Is the Starting Point

A. *Being and consciousness:* Despite brilliant and profound works, all attempts of the older metaphysics to arrive at a direct formulation of being that would be valid for all men proved vain. Kant hoped to find solid ground if he started from what is manifested to every man who strives to know. Being remains the central interest. But in order to apprehend it clearly and without deception, we must approach it in the area where it manifests itself. That area is our existence.

Our existence is consciousness. Elucidation of consciousness is elucidation of our thinking. My existence is a being that knows of something and of itself. In regard to its intention, the elucidation of consciousness as thinking applies not to me as an individual but to "consciousness as such," to the "I" that is every I. But the being of objects signifies that they can be known.

What in existence I cannot think away without negating existence, is the categories, which give all things the form of objects. Nothing exists for us unless the forms of thought are presupposed. Without them there is no objectivity, we are without consciousness and can no longer speak. It is only this origin of all objectivity, this one source in the "I think," that throws light on space and time. Only the categorical is all-encompassing.

B. *What should we take as our starting point in this area of thought, to which we are restricted in our thinking?* In this area we find what thought has already produced: language, statement, judgments; functions of thought, objects; subjectivity, objectivity. Beginning with any of these phenomena, the inquiry will ultimately move in the circle to which thinking itself confines us in our thinking. For in thinking about thinking itself, we presuppose thinking and in trying to know what knowledge is, we presuppose knowledge.

Kant starts from the knowledge at hand. We claim correctness for our judgments. In the sciences such judgments are presented in coherent systems. Kant inquires into the judgments and their justification. He starts, not from the objects of cognition but from the cognitive process as manifested in judgments. But though accented, this is only one of his starting points.

C. *The trial:* Insofar as he takes this starting point, Kant asks after the objective validity of our cognition. He then undertakes to justify this objective validity. His exposition takes the form of a trial.

The dogmatists have set up many assertions and proofs, empirical, mathematical, metaphysical. They are opposed by the plaintiffs, the skeptics, who say: These are mere opinions, grown out of habit, modes of belief that are useful in practice. Kant seeks to arbitrate the dispute. Both parties, he perceives, assume that there are objects as such and that the cognitive subject comes to them, in order to know them correctly or incorrectly. The dispute cannot be settled by a compromise, but only by the insight that the presupposition of both parties is false. All previous theories of knowledge must be abandoned: the notion that things themselves flow into the subject by way of images; that things are copied in corresponding representations; that the Creator has pre-established a harmony between objective happening and subjective thinking. Kant's insight that we know things because we produce them in respect to their form through consciousness as such justifies the validity of knowledge: we know what we ourselves, "the subject as such," have created. Then the concordance is no longer a problem. Neither the dogmatic metaphysicians nor the skeptics were right. The case is decided in favor of neither of the two parties. Court is dismissed because the critical philosophy has contributed new evidence.

D. *Conceptions of the subject:* If being as existence is consciousness and if consciousness is cognition, then everything we know is knowable only in this situation of existence. Let us look a little more closely: What is the cognitive subject (which Kant calls consciousness as such, the spontaneity of thought, the unity of synthesis in the act of thought, or transcendental apperception)?

It is not the individual, but the "I think," the *cogito* of "consciousness as such." The validity of our judgments is based not on accidental opinion, but on the categories inherent in the "I think." They are the source of objects and of the knowledge of objects, as it exists for every finite thinking consciousness. They single out the valid from the stream of becoming in the manifold of subjects, as that which pertains to the one consciousness as such that is common to them all.

Hence the subject of consciousness as such is not the empirical psychological subject, which I can observe and investigate. It is not accessible to self-observation but only to self-certainty. It does not exist objectively as something other, but is present in the operation. I myself, in knowing, am this consciousness as such, which knows, but is not itself known as an object. This is the point that distinguishes it from every mere object. In my knowing, knowledge and being are not separate, but identical.

What I psychologically observe and inwardly perceive as my subjectivity exists only through the intention of the *cogito* which directs the inner sense toward this field. What I outwardly and inwardly perceive belongs equally to the objective world, and the same is true of my thought processes insofar as they are accessible to psychological observation.

It is a mistake to suppose that all existence is divided into external things and inner (psychic) subjectivity. This applies to everything I observe but not to the source of my observation, the "I think" of the all-encompassing consciousness as such, for which both outward and inward become an object, though it does not itself become one. In our thinking, it is a constructed point, which utterly eludes observation but forms a certainty in our self-consciousness. It would be a mistake to identify myself with the way in which I appear to other men's psychological observation or my own. Beyond it, I am the essentially so mysterious *cogito,* which is the source of all lucidity.

Once again: in the cognitive act of my self-consciousness, I do not gain knowledge of myself as a particular object. In objective knowledge of myself, I consider my existence psychologically, taking it as an object. But now I pass beyond this objectivization and return to the active knowledge of my self-consciousness. The more this knowledge identifies itself with thinking, the more it eludes psychological observation. In thinking, I know that I am, but only that I am and not how I appear to myself in the fullness of my being-given to myself as this psychological individual, nor what I as the foundation of myself am.

This awareness of being in the "I think" is something quite remarkable. The consciousness of my empirical existence in time must be expressly distinguished from the consciousness of my timeless "I think." The "I think" does not itself become the object of an "intellectual intuition," but remains a mere self-certainty because, having no existence accessible to temporal intuition, it is timeless and eludes our grasp. All inner intuition (like outward intuition) is subject to the condition of time. If there were such a thing as intellectual intuition, it would have to apprehend the timelessness of the "I think" and the "I am." That is not possible.

To be sure, our consciousness of our own existence is connected with the "I think." Everything that exists for us is actualized by its connection with our existence and so takes on an existence of its own. Thus Kant, in speaking of the starry heavens above and the ethical law within, says: "I relate them directly to my being aware of my own existence." But this link with my existence as a thinking subject tells me nothing about my individual subject. The self-certainty of existence in the "I think" permits no valid statement about the substance of my I, or, consequently, about its immortality, unity, uniqueness. All it gives me is the punctual being of the "I think."

On the other hand, the "I think" is all-encompassing. Everything that discloses itself directly or indirectly as being must be manifested in consciousness as such. I apprehend the fundamental possibilities of being insofar as it is accessible to valid knowledge, by elucidating the elements of consciousness as such.

The concept of the subject is a leading theme in modern philosophy. Descartes grounded his thinking in the pure self-certainty of the *cogito ergo sum*. Locke conceived the subject as something which is initially without content and draws all its content from experience—as a *tabula rasa* on which an outside agent writes. Leibniz regarded the subject as a monad, filled from the very outset with the entire content of the cosmos, which in it develops from unconsciousness to consciousness, from disorder to clarity. Hume's subject was a bundle of representations, which comes into being through the accidents of experience and deludes itself with such pseudo objectivizations as I, substance, causality. Kant's view of the subject was more profound. He distinguished: first, the empirical subject as an object of psychological observation; second, the pure consciousness of the "I think" as the source of valid knowledge; third, the intelligible character as the source of freedom (of which we shall speak later on).

E. *Recapitulation and anticipation:* Have we properly understood all this? So far we have given a rather dogmatic summary of what is known as Kant's theory of knowledge. But the way in which Kant derives the forms of all empirical knowledge is by no means self-explanatory. It is by no means clear how the subject produces the object in respect to its form. Perhaps, in our effort to follow and understand, there has been an element of good will that made us shut our eyes to what we have failed to grasp. Our failure to understand requires clarification. Perhaps an understanding of our own nonunderstanding will bring us closer to the idea underlying this whole "theory of knowledge."

Let us recall the insuperable difficulty inherent in the very nature of Kant's thinking. He questions the subject-object dichotomy, yet every question and every answer must be situated within it. For every something is thought by a thinker. Kant wishes to think beyond the dichotomy to the ground from which it springs, but he can do so only by means of categories and objectivizations which themselves belong to the dichotomy. This is the inevitable difficulty and the greatness of Kant—he does not abandon himself to the mystical ecstasy of incommunicable unthinkables. Remaining within the lucidity of the natural consciousness, he enters into relationships which, though thinkable, conceal something that is unthinkable, yet indirectly disclose it and thus, within the confines of consciousness, touch upon the ground and root of consciousness.

Kant himself referred to this only occasionally, and did not develop the underlying thought with fundamental clarity. With his wealth of intellectual invention, he carried out operations which elucidate the subject-object dichotomy in all directions, but he did not reflect on how he did so. Thus his work is a tissue of movements of thought, which can indeed be disentangled, but which retain their force only when taken as a whole. Each separate operation is very clear, but in the whole there is a necessary unclarity. Consequently, despite the conceptual refinement that makes Kant's work a masterpiece, the work itself must be carried back to the source of his philosophy. For what is crucial in the work is not the particular operations, but something at which they aim though they never capture it. No thematic conclusion is reached. The true achievement is not an objective system of thought but a fundamental revolution in thinking, which, though it is achieved by conceptual operations, cannot be defined with final clarity.

The Kantian revolution in philosophy is expressed in the formulation of problems none of which can be considered as the only or ultimate question. Kant states his thought in the form of definite questions and answers, preserving the traditional manner of formulating philosophical problems because without it he would have been able neither to advance his own understanding nor to communicate it. But in Kant—as in Plato and Augustine—the problems themselves are transcended in an all-encompassing field. Through his formulation of the problems we can attain to the source of the problems; this is the goal which, surpassing themselves and their answers, they seek to attain.

7. *The Transcendental Deduction*

The "Transcendental Deduction," which is the central section of the *Critique of Pure Reason,* deals with relations between subject and object in so intricate a way that, though particular insights are perfectly clear, the unintelligible character of the whole seems to stand out as the essential fact. Several questions are treated simultaneously: How is thought related to the object? What happens in cognition? What is the reality of the object? What is the source of the objectivity of valid judgments? This last question is the explicit theme: Kant sets out to deduce the justification of the validity of empirical judgments. But what is experience? All these questions are combined in one comprehensive question that can be formulated only very vaguely: What is being? and in the equally indeterminate answer: As it appears to us in the phenomenality of our existence.

A. *Deduction:* Deduction means derivation, grounding, justification. Kant is referring to the grounding of the objective validity of a priori concepts. First he excludes from his discussion the "psychological" or "empirical deduction," according to which representations come into being as reactions of the mind to external things. That was Locke's concern, not Kant's. Then he differentiates between the "metaphysical deduction" of the categories from the universal logical functions of thought (the judgments) and "transcendental deduction," that is, the explanation of the way in which a priori concepts can relate to objects. Transcendental deduction is concerned not with matters of empirical fact (*quid facti*) but with the justification of validity (*quid juris*). Within the transcendental deduction, Kant further differentiates an objective deduction whose purpose it is to explain the validity of a priori concepts—it provides an answer to the question: What can the understanding know without experience?—and a subjective deduction, which considers the pure understanding itself according to its cognitive powers—it provides an answer to the question: How is the faculty of thinking possible?

B. *The fundamental idea in the form of an alternative argumentation:* Let us outline Kant's brief argumentation on the question: How does it come about that our experience accords with our concepts of its objects? There are two ways of conceiving this necessary agreement: either experience makes possible the concepts or the concepts make possible the experience. A middle course would be to maintain that there is a pre-established harmony between our subjective thinking, implanted in us by the Creator, and the objective laws of nature. Kant rejects this middle course, for to take it is to lose sight of the first a priori principles of knowledge—our judgments would lack

necessity—and before even attempting an insight, to resign oneself to understanding nothing.

After excluding the middle course, we still have an alternative. But if we
say that it is experience which first makes possible the concepts, there is no
way of understanding how we make necessary and universally valid judgments in respect to the objects of experience, for judgments would be valid
only insofar as they are supported by experience. This actually holds good
for material empiric judgments. But these in turn are made possible only
by universal and necessary judgments concerning the lawfulness of experience in general. Before we can determine specific laws, we must establish
the law that all nature is subject to law, that everything I experience is subject to some form of law, which I discover in connection with experience,
but not through experience alone. For this necessity of law is the a priori
source of all the forms of the objects that appear to me. It is the source of
all my empirical judgments, which are not annulled by new experience but
completed and gathered into wider concepts. Because there are necessary
and universally valid empirical judgments, we must therefore accept the other
thesis. This thesis, which seems absurd at first sight, is Kant's discovery:
Necessary and universally valid empirical judgments are possible only because our concepts, instead of being derived from sense perception, have first
built up the objects in respect to their form.

c. *An expressly limited theme and its actual scope:* The "transcendental deduction" is the core of Kant's *Critique of Pure Reason,* the foundation of
the whole critical edifice. Its exposition is almost inextricably complex, and
moreover it is set forth in two very different versions (the first and second
editions of the *Critique*).

The explicit aim is to justify the validity of our empirical knowledge. The
actual content is far wider, covering the whole nature of our thinking and
cognition. But let us examine Kant's method more closely.

8. *Analysis of Kant's Methods of Clarifying the Original Source Which Is Beyond the Object*

To interpret Kant's thought as meaning that the world is produced by the
subjectivity of man's mental constitution or the condition of his brain is to
reduce it to absurdity. There is a temptation to make it so simple in order
to understand it and then reject what has thus been understood. But even
Kant's brief formulation of his fundamental idea is extraordinarily complex,
as he himself was well aware. This, he tells us, was the section that had
given him the most trouble, and he expresses the hope that his pains will not
go unrewarded. For a better understanding, let us recall the general character of this thinking.

Kant knows that his thinking surpasses, "transcends," natural thinking.

The use of the word in the sense of philosophical transcending has a long history that goes back to Augustine. Kant gives it a new meaning: "I entitle *transcendental* all knowledge which is occupied not so much with objects as with the mode of our knowledge of objects insofar as this mode of knowledge is to be possible a priori." The old dogmatic metaphysics, thinking in the objective world, transcended it to arrive at a supersensible object, at pure being or God. Kant transcends objective thinking backward, as it were, seeking to arrive at the condition of all objectivity. His goal is no longer the metaphysical knowledge of another world, but knowledge of the origin of our knowledge. Instead of seeking the origin of all things, he seeks the origin of the subject-object dichotomy. The end is not an object to be known as in the older metaphysics but an awareness of the limits of our knowledge.

The fundamental difficulty is that Kant, in striving to disclose the conditions of all objectivity, is compelled to operate within objective thinking itself, hence in a realm of objects which must not be treated as objects. He tries to understand the subject-object relationship in which we live as though it were possible to be outside it. He strives toward the limits of the existence of all being for us; standing at the limit, he endeavors to perceive the origin of the whole, but he must always remain within the limit. With his transcendental method he strives to transcend while remaining within the world. He thinks about thought. Yet he cannot do so from outside of thought, but only by thinking.

A. *The four guiding threads of Kant's thought:* In this brief space it is not possible to reproduce the intricate development of Kant's ideas. But we can show their structure. We find that Kant follows *four* paths of exemplifying exposition. He speaks "psychologically" in dealing with consciousness, the action of the subject, imagination; "logically" in dealing with unity, form and matter, judgment, validity; "methodologically" in dealing with the prerequisites of knowledge, the condition of the possibility of experience, with anticipation and purposive design, the knowledge of what I can do; "metaphysically" in dealing with the thing in itself as it affects the subject, with the inner sense and its affective knowledge of the self.

In his differentiation of the four, he holds to traditional and well-established "departments" or "disciplines" of philosophy. With this schema I do not pretend to give a complete picture of the Kantian concepts or to say that the four points of view are equivalent in value. Some concepts can be assigned to several departments. A systematic study of Kant's texts from these points of view would clarify certain matters, but it would also show the questionable nature of the differentiation. They offer provisional answers to the question. But the question remains: By what operations can I penetrate to Kant's meaning? We term psychological the investigation of experience; logical, that of thought in respect to the structure and meaning of judgments; methodological, the study of the procedure employed by science in discovering facts and laws; and metaphysical, the investigation of being conceived as an object, but raised to the level of being as such, that is, of an absolute.

But to perceive the radiance of Kant's philosophical idea, we must carry it through in a single act. If any of the guiding threads of Kant's thinking is taken for the thought itself, we have a falsification. By way of countering such falsifications, we may formulate them as four misunderstandings. They all have a Kantian foundation, but in isolation they are no longer Kantian.

The *psychological misunderstanding* would express the Kantian ideas as follows: Our human organization with its synthetizing understanding reacts to the impressions that enter into consciousness by creating the outside world as a fiction of our human consciousness. From this standpoint we can engage in empirical, psychological investigations of sense perception, which, however, itself presupposes objectivity as such and categories.

The *logical misunderstanding* can be framed in the following formula: The confrontation is not between sensation and a spontaneous understanding but between matter and the form in which it is encompassed. The structure of objects consists in the relation between form and matter. The terms "form" and "matter"—according to this view—clearly describe the situation, whereas all others, the psychological or metaphysical, result in falsification. A valid form embraces matter—thereby objects are present. Objectivity is the product of nonsensuous, universal form and the matter it embraces. The validity, the logical claim, is absolute. Here the subject-object relation is lost, the thing in itself becomes a superfluous concept.

The *methodological misunderstanding* says: In its design the understanding anticipates what it knows in experience. But since by its anticipatory schema it has created experience in respect to its form, it merely finds again in experience what it has itself created. With this the method of true empirical knowledge, which tests its cogitated designs by experience and proceeds to reject or confirm them, is made into the foundation of objectivity and of the whole intelligible world.

The *metaphysical misunderstanding* is roughly as follows: Things in themselves affect the "consciousness as such." Their interaction gives rise, in our empirical consciousness, to the world of appearances and of experience. From the fact of experience we deduce these two transcendent points as absolute realities: on the one hand, the thing in itself; on the other, consciousness as such.

On each of the four paths I can conclude that I am in the totality to which everything real and valid for me must belong. And yet in every case I am engaged in a particular mode of interpreting the intelligible; in every case I am involved in the paradox of a universal particularity.

When we examine the various interpretations of Kant, we find that one of the four perspectives is always accented or taken exclusively. But anyone who takes one of these seemingly clear interpretations as the correct one and attempts to interpret and correct the Kantian text in accordance with it, finds himself hard pressed. He cannot do what he set out to; statements favoring one of the other perspectives keep cropping up. All sorts of statements can be found in Kant; he even said that the world is conditioned "by our brain." Kant himself seems to have expressed all the distortions of Kantianism. Consequently, the one-sided interpreters are forever correcting Kant by himself, that is, on the strength of the one guiding thread that they take to be the right one. The psychological, logical, methodological, metaphysical views all lead to the common error; they all treat as a finite object what can only be understood by an operation of philosophical transcendence. Though indispensable to the philosophical meaning as a whole, these objectivizations kill it when retained as such.

The Deduction, considered in all the texts relating to it, is not a closed system but a broad movement of logically limited operations; it circles around itself, gathers up relatively self-contained operations, none of which however has the right meaning or any independent existence if taken by itself.

On each of the four paths, it seems possible to understand something definite and clear. Having grasped it, one supposes that one has understood Kant. But Kant's meaning cuts across all these modes of expression; it is a virtual point around which they all circle. Thus all the modes of expression require a translation, not into something else that can be stated directly, but into an awareness of the Encompassing, through which all these definite formulations first acquire their meaning.

Kant himself repeatedly calls for this method by expressly insisting on an abrupt transition to the transcendental and by translating his statements from one mode of expression into another. The reader can easily become confused until his very confusion gives rise to the clarity that can be apprehended in none of the definite objective statements.

Only taken together as one context can the four paths communicate Kant's transcendental meaning. Since Kant keeps his goal firmly in mind, he employs the method we have described, though he never formulates it explicitly: Since all objective expression is inappropriate to what cannot be grasped in objective terms, but since in any given moment we can think only objectively, Kant passes successively from one to another of the four possible modes of expression, each of which he annuls by the next. By weaving them all together, he prevents the discerning reader from holding fast to any definite idea, and thus enables him, through the intricate web of always inadequate representations, to arrive indirectly at the central meaning.

B. *Tautology, vicious circle, contradiction:* A second characteristic of Kant's method—again not explicitly stated but carried through in practice—is the logical discrepancy that serves a very good and necessary purpose.

What must I do if I wish to gain awareness of the Encompassing? With the help of clear insights I must go beyond them; I must let my clear insights collapse, like ladders that I no longer need once I have climbed to a certain height.

This I do *first* in the way already discussed: I draw each of the guiding threads into a combination with the others, so that while each thread is necessary to the whole tissue, it cannot in itself represent the meaning of the whole.

A *second* reason for this dropping of ladders is that this mode of thinking does not lend itself to objective logic. The nonobject which is to be elucidated as the source of all objectivity (subject-object dichotomy) cannot be encompassed in objective terms and yet can only be thought objectively. Consequently, what is conceived in this way, if it is not to be fixated as a false object, must culminate in formal failure, that is, in tautologies, vicious circles, and contradictions.

Tautology means a statement that is implicit in the subject; it is not false, but it adds no knowledge. A vicious circle occurs when I base a statement not on something else but on itself; it is not false except insofar as it pretends to supply a justification. Contradiction occurs when propositions negate one another; it means untenability.

It is generally true of philosophy based on a transcending idea that logical forms cannot adequately state what it is aiming at. The more intense the logical effort, the more purely the idea that shatters the logical form is expressed. It is impossible to set forth a construction of being or even, as in Kant, a construction of being as it is disclosed to cognition, in a system free from contradiction.

In connection with every transcending philosophy, we must ask what form of logical impossibility the fundamental idea has run into. In Kant the question applies to his transcendental logic. First a few examples:

1. Obvious *contradictions:* Kant circles round the noumenon (the intelligible, the thing in itself) by means of negations. The noumenon is without sensuous qualities, space and time, or categories. Hence our idea of it does not partake of knowledge. Objectively its content is nothing. Yet this nothing figures as something. The void has a content.

"Cause" is a category, hence it applies only to phenomena. Hence the "thing in itself" cannot be a cause. But Kant calls it the cause of phenomena and so contradicts himself. Similarly Kant speaks later on of freedom as an "intelligible cause" which, although it is not itself determined by phenomena, manifests their effects. But causality, thing, reality are regarded as categories only of phenomena. If the relation of the thing in itself to our understanding and our cognition is subordinated to the category of causality, the thing in itself ceases to be "in itself" and becomes a phenomenon.

For Kant the thing in itself is indispensable as a complement to the phenomenon, "for otherwise we should have the absurd proposition that there is appearance without anything that appears." The relation of the "in itself" to appearance is in itself a contradiction.

Kant conceives the thing in itself, or noumenon, as a "limiting concept" free from all the categorial determinations of the object. But in thinking the limit I am already beyond it. By showing that it is impossible to surpass the limit of the concept, Kant effects this impossible operation. "Thing in itself" is an apter term than "noumenon," because it directly implies the contradiction. Only a phenomenon can be conceived as a "thing"; "in itself" means that it is not a phenomenon. "Noumenon" means what is thought, but what is thought in it is unthinkable.

Phenomenon and thing in itself are untenable notions from the standpoint of objective knowledge, but in their failure they are indispensable. If they are taken as tangible entities, they lead to a distortion. Two worlds arise, one in the foreground, the other in the background. The two are related but each seems to have a separate existence of its own. The background world becomes a realm of phantasms, whose contents all stem from our world. But for Kant there is only one world. What is touched upon in transcending thought is not another world, but no world at all. And insofar as it exists, it exists in this nonworld. A theory of two worlds is not Kantian, but only an inevitably contradictory mode of expression.

2. In Kant's fundamental ideas we find *vicious circles*. The validity of the principles of cognition is to be demonstrated. It springs from the function of thinking which produces the unity of the object. Psychologically speaking, empirical apperception by empirical synthesis creates subjective, not objectively valid unities, from the manifold of sensation. Transcendentally speaking, transcendental apperception by pure syntheses creates objectively valid objects from the manifold of given matter. What is the difference between these two unifying functions? The mode of validity of the unities they form. Empirical apperception creates only subjectively valid unities, such as the association of a concept with a particular word or the habitual combinations resulting from the accidents of subjective experience. Transcendental apperception creates objectively valid unities "in accordance with a rule." There is no other difference between transcendental and empirical synthesis. But what does this mean? We follow Kant's proof of the validity of empirical knowledge. It is valid, we learn, because it comes into being in accordance with the condition of transcendental synthesis, that is, according to a rule. But objective validity was already a characteristic of transcendental synthesis. In short: experience is valid because its transcendental factors of unity are valid. Or: it is valid because it is valid. The only way to justify universal validity is to presuppose it.

But here perhaps we have merely isolated one aspect of Kant's argument, which is not intended as a demonstration. The core of the matter, we are told, lies deeper. In seeking it we run into another kind of logical fallacy.

Suppose we interpret and say that Kant's main purpose is not a justification of validity, that the distinction between subjective and objective validity is mentioned only in passing, and that Kant's primary aim is to elucidate the possibility of valid knowledge by showing that not only the knowledge of objects but objects themselves in their objectivity are first made possible by the transcendental synthesis of the understanding, that is, through the categories. To grasp this possibility is to justify the validity of categorial synthesis in knowledge.

But what does "possible" mean here? We know logical possibilities as freedom from contradiction; we know material possibility as the sum of the causes that condition an event. We regard as possible what can happen, but does not have to. But these cannot be the possibilities meant in the Transcendental Deduction. For they are particular and formulable. They are possibilities taken as categories. But in the philosophical idea what is meant is a transcendental possibility. With this magic word—a category that can no longer be a category—we are expected to tear ourselves loose from the categories in order to perceive the origin of all categories. In Kant's view, to be sure, we cannot by means of our knowledge transcend into a supernatural world, but we can gain awareness of the source of all objectivity. In this process the understanding must always operate with the categories, here the category of "possibility," but not with any particular, determinate possibility. We are left with the contradiction between the transcendental possibility and every determinate possibility.

To avoid the vicious circle in our interpretation, we have invited contradiction.

3. Kant's fundamental ideas are *tautologies*. Nietzsche criticizes Kant for answering the question: What makes knowledge possible? with the tautology: The faculty of knowledge. He accuses Kant of hiding this tautology beneath a mass of Teutonic circumlocutions and profundities. Yet Nietzsche might have quoted a sentence in which Kant does not hide the tautology at all but states it quite openly: "The possibility of the logical form of all knowledge is necessarily based on its relation to this apperception as a faculty." Nietzsche's argument is superficially correct but shows an utter lack of understanding for the method of a philosophizing that seeks clarification through transcending.

The compendious literature on Kant has disclosed numerous contradictions, vicious circles, and tautologies. Among them we must distinguish between those that are inherent in the underlying thought and the few incidental, nonessential mistakes. The literature can be exceedingly helpful, for where it claims to refute, it provides pointers to true understanding.

There is a greatness in Kant's vicious circles and tautologies: they open up a path to every aspect of philosophical consciousness. The vicious circle, for example, takes as many forms as Kant requires modes of expression— whether psychological, logical, methodological—in contradistinction to the linearity and tedious rigidity of the one vicious circle characteristic of spurious philosophical endeavors. Moreover, the vicious circles necessary for the elucidation of cognition form only one group. Others arise as Kant goes on to the philosophy of freedom, the beautiful, history, and politics.

It is not as though vicious circles, tautologies, and contradictions could be avoided in philosophizing. They mark the difference between philosophical and scientific knowledge. Philosophical knowledge is directed toward the whole which has nothing outside it, scientific knowledge toward definite objects that confront other objects. Philosophical knowledge strives to transcend all presuppositions in order to preserve its openness to the whole; scientific knowledge derives its cogency from presuppositions and operates in the realm of determinate, particular experience. However, in taking as its object what is no longer an object but the encompassing whole, a realm where the only presupposition is a complete absence of presuppositions, philosophy inevitably runs into vicious circles, tautologies, and contradictions, because it strives to perceive the whole through the whole, not through something else, and to understand its own thinking through itself, not through something that went before. Logic is bound to break down whenever an attempt is made to think something that cannot be appropriately framed in the forms of logic. Such thinking necessitates a circling-around-itself and contradiction.

Kant's thinking aims not at objective knowledge but at self-certainty in the realm of objective knowledge. In striving to attain clarity concerning itself and to express itself, it requires concepts. It can employ them only by making at every step a logical mistake; but in effacing the logical errors, it gains lucidity and succeeds in jumping over its own shadow. We can understand the prison of objectivity and phenomenality only by going beyond it; but every thought puts us back in it again.

This is why it is not possible to capture Kant's philosophical ideas as results like the findings of the specialized sciences. The idea is never a definite result—the results are the vicious circles, tautologies, contradictions—but derives its value only from an act of awareness of being. Like all philosophy —and unlike compelling scientific insight—it is not an object of universal acceptance; it is not understood identically by many. Where the act of awareness is not repeated, the idea passes away, ceasing to be anything more than a *caput mortuum* of in themselves rather strange propositions that need only to be learned. If we take Kant's ideas literally, we can recite his words and torment ourselves indefinitely over contradictions and misconceptions we should not fall into—but we gain neither a compelling insight (though we may like to think so) nor a philosophical meaning that transforms our awareness of being. For that we need something else: for a philosophical understanding of such ideas we must tear ourselves away from particular objects and ideas and enact Kant's knowledge of the phenomenality of the whole insofar as it is objective, spatial, temporal, cogitated. Then, in my philosophizing, I shall experience the idea that gave rise to the vicious circles, tautologies, and contradictions, and, looking on as these structures are consumed in the flames of logical annihilation, I shall, through them, gain clarity in regard to my existential situation.

The fundamental ground of truth is the soaring of the philosophical awareness of being to achieve a broad vision of everything that discloses itself to us as being, or it is the presence of the depths whence everything that is for us and everything we are draws its being. This incomprehensible truth is the force which compels us to cast off the vicious circles, tautologies, and contradictions it produces. It tears us out of the context of every particular objective thought and helps us to come to ourselves. This alone is the philosophical act. Only when the whole thought remains within the sphere of scientific argumentation is the vicious circle a mistake that destroys the meaning. But a philosophical impulse can elucidate itself in the form of a fundamental knowledge only if the particular argumentation logically negates itself and so permits the content of the philosophical act to shine forth.

c. *The phenomenological, constructive, argumentative methods:* In considering one by one the methods which Kant actually used all together, we must (after the four guiding threads and the forms of logical fallacy) take up a third point of view. The quality of evidence rests either on phenomenological observation or on a construction which reproduces, as it were, the hidden structures and processes of our reason, or on argumentations which decide between possibilities on the basis of concepts and their consequences. These modes of evidence are employed by turns and together; hence they cannot be decisive when taken singly.

The *phenomenological* method leads to intuitive certainty by mere observation. For example: we cannot represent a world without space. Whatever we represent is represented in space. We can think every object away, we can think of a space without objects. There always remain space and my thinking self. Another example: Kant considers what would be if there were no thinking but only sensation: chaos, confusion, less than a dream. And he considers what would be if only the understanding determined its objects and there were no reason to set the task of creating systematic unity through ideas; then there would be an infinity of dispersed objects, without relation to a unity forming them into a systematic whole; thus there would be no possibility of science.

Another example: our aesthetic judgments imply a feeling that is determined solely by beauty without interest in the reality either of an object to be used, or of action good or bad.

Constructively, Kant outlines the stages in the formation of the object, from the synthesis of apprehension in intuition to the synthesis of recognition in the concept. He discloses the process by which all objects possible for us are framed in space, time, and categories.

Constructively, he situates the function of the imagination between understanding and intuition. Everywhere he seeks the middle factor.

Constructively Kant considers judgments of taste as the "free play of the cognitive faculties." He finds this free play in the "concordance of all our faculties to form any cognition whatever."

Kant proceeds *argumentatively* in discussing the possible ways in which knowledge can relate to an object and in justifying the decision between them.

Another example: Kant starts from the fact of science and asks what makes it possible. From the fact that our mathematical knowledge—for example, our knowledge of the triangle that we find in pure intuitive thinking—applies to experience though it is not taken from experience, he concludes that all objects we encounter in reality were previously (a priori) formed by the functions of the mathematical understanding.

Still another example: from the fact that "judgments of taste" lay claim to universal validity, Kant concludes that such judgments are based on "the subjective factor which can be presupposed in all men (as necessary for all possible knowledge)."

In these cases the fact of universal validity is justified by an argumentation based on a construction of its source.

We separate the methods in order to examine the particular character of each one. But this is not to accuse Kant of confusion. On the contrary, the depth of his fundamental philosophical idea lies precisely in the involvement of his method, or better still, in the fact that all the aspects we thus clarify belong to an idea which itself cannot be elucidated as a determinate, particular idea. When we unravel these methods, we are left with a number of philosophically ineffectual parts. The fundamental idea cannot be defined by any method. We must beware of considering any of the particular ideas, that are mere aspects, as the fundamental idea, or to reject it singly. For it is only in their interplay that the truth of the philosophical insight is disclosed.

9. *The Antinomies*

When Kant noted: "The year '69 gave me great light," he was thinking of his method of discovering the antinomies. Here was an independent point of departure for transcendental thinking based on critique. The doctrine of the antinomies remained an independent part and ran like an effective form through his subsequent critical works. It might have been a more dramatic beginning for Kant's work than the question: How are synthetic a priori judgments possible?

A. *Kant's method of discovery:* It was generally known that the central propositions of the metaphysicians contradicted one another. The new element was that Kant systematically sought out these contradictions, that he

carefully and with equal evidence carried out the proofs of mutually contradictory propositions, and then asked how this all-encompassing illusion
might be accounted for by the nature of our cognitive faculty.

Here are some of his antinomies: (1) Thesis: The world has a beginning
in time and is enclosed in spatial boundaries. Antithesis: The world has
no beginning and no limits in space, but is infinite in space and time. (2)
Thesis: Every composite substance in the world consists of simple elements;
nothing exists but simple elements and what is composed of them. Antithesis:
No composite thing in the world consists of simple elements; there
is nowhere any simple element. (3) Thesis: Natural causality is not the
only causality from which all phenomena in the world can be derived. Another causality based on freedom is also necessary to explain them. Antithesis:
There is no freedom; rather, everything in the world happens solely
in accordance with natural causality.

B. *An example of a proof:* The world has a beginning in time. Let us
assume the opposite, that it has no beginning. Then, up to any given point
in time, an infinite sequence of successive states must have elapsed. But
infinity means that the sequence can never be completed. Thus an infinite
sequence can never be completed. Thus an infinite sequence of past states
is impossible. Hence a beginning of the world is the necessary condition of
its present existence. Q.E.D.

All these proofs are indirect; they demonstrate through the impossibility
of their contrary. Since thesis alternates with antithesis, the last speaker is
always right.

Kant's proofs—in large part recapitulations of demonstrations actually put
forward in the course of the history of philosophy—have been criticized in
detail. Critics have found fallacies. But Kant himself regarded the demonstrations as false. Hence the only relevant question is whether there are
other fallacies than those recognized by Kant. But this makes no change in
the general picture.

Let us examine the first proof more closely. The word "elapsed" implies
that the temporal sequence of states of the world includes the flow of time
into the future (progression). A reversal of the direction makes the proof
false. "Never completed," meaning: Going backward, we never arrive at
a beginning, is reversed to mean: The sequence is complete in every now.
The proposition that the beginning is never attained is refuted by the very
different proposition that the present point in time is attained.

But that is Kant's own opinion. He sets forth the proofs not as his own
proofs, but as a way of showing that a thinking which operates solely with
concepts becomes involved in hopeless antinomies. In conceptual abstraction
divorced from intuition, it is quite natural to identify the regressive and the
progressive sequences of time; the distinction which obviates the false reversal requires intuition of temporal progression.

The proof may be formulated in another way: What has an end must have a beginning. But the temporal sequence of states of the world contains, in every point of time, an end to what has gone before. Therefore the world must have a beginning in time. Or in still another formulation: If the past time of the world's existence were infinite, then everything that is possible must already have happened. No progress would be possible but only repetition, that is, the beginning and end of new cycles, or death in a final state that must have occurred long ago.

However, Kant does not consider these indirect proofs of thesis and antithesis as a sophistical game. To his mind they disclose a natural contradiction inherent in our reason. He takes it as his task to let the contradiction develop to the full, in order that he may understand it as an error following necessarily from its source and so find a way of correcting it. This skeptical method by which Kant brilliantly lets a large part of the traditional metaphysics destroy itself, is, he says, limited to transcendental philosophy. It exists neither in mathematics nor in experimental physics. But it is this skeptical method that leads him to a solid ground of certainty.

c. *Kant's procedure:* Hence we must examine Kant's procedure as a whole: the source of the antinomies, the solution of the antinomies, and finally, the significance of this insight for our awareness of being as a whole.

1. In view of the antinomies, that is, the never-ending quarrels of the traditional metaphysics, it occurred to Kant that something must be amiss and that the difficulty lay, not in any particular mistakes, but in intelligibility as such, in the structure of our reason itself.

Antinomies arise when our thinking advances from what is given in intuition to what is not given but disclosed to us as the condition of the given; when, secondly, the sum of these not-given conditions is conceived as a completed whole, that is, when the sum of these conditions is conceived as culminating in the unconditional; and when, thirdly, this whole (the totality of conditions, the unconditional) is represented by reason as an object and endowed with objective reality.

This "transcending"—as Kant puts it—from understanding to reason is the source of the antinomies. Kant distinguishes between understanding, which proceeds to empirical knowledge through certain concepts whose contents can be actualized in intuition, and reason which by inferences and conclusions passes beyond what can be intuitively actualized and thus arrives at a totality, at the idea of the world as a whole. In understanding, only particular empirical knowledge is gained; reason strives for completeness. From understanding as a faculty spring the categories of definite objects; from reason as a faculty spring the Ideas of a nonobjective, indeterminate totality.

Reason is right in holding that the sum of all the conditions of what we experience in actual intuition forms an absolutely complete totality. But what it represents is only an Idea, not an object. It is wrong when it makes the world into an object. The world is not an object; rather, all objects are in the world. But the world is a true Idea.

Total experience of the totality can be gained neither through direct sensibility nor imagination, but only through the concepts of reason, to which no object corresponds because they are incapable of intuitive realization. But the aspiration to *absolute* totality does not mean that such a totality is given or attainable, or even that it is thinkable.

Consequently, if a natural tendency of our thinking leads us to attempt the impossible, to transform the content of an idea of reason into a concept of the understanding, the inevitable result is contradiction: thesis and antithesis. If the totality is conceived in conformity with the unity of reason—if, for example, we say that the world is infinite in respect to space and time—it becomes too large for the understanding. If the totality is conceived in conformity with the understanding—the world is finite in space and time—it becomes too small for reason. Reason is bound to make things too big for the understanding, and the understanding to make them too little for reason. The beginning in time, the finiteness of the world in space, the simplest indivisible particle—all are too little. Whereas a world without a beginning, spatial infinity, an infinity of infinitely divisible particles—all these are too big.

All demonstrations that go beyond what can be experienced in sensory intuition are attempts to provide compelling knowledge of objective reality through mere concepts. And this is impossible.

The proofs which show through antinomies that the understanding goes astray when it takes the Ideas of reason as an object, involve intuitions: either they present a positive intuition of the beginning and end of things and events in the world (finite forms carried over into the totality), or they call for an intuitive operation that is impossible (representation of a limit beyond which there is no space and time). Then, since the limit cannot be represented, it is inferred that the world is infinite. The alternate application and rejection of intuition, followed by logical operations with pure concepts, creates an illusion of evidence.

The total object, "the world," can never occur in experience. "In all our possible perceptions," says Kant, "we always remain involved in conditions, whether in space or in time, and come upon nothing unconditioned requiring us to determine whether this unconditioned is to be located in an absolute beginning of synthesis, or in an absolute totality of a series that has no beginning. In its empirical meaning, the term 'whole' is always only comparative. The absolute whole of quantity (the universe), the whole of division, of derivation, of the condition of existence in general . . . have nothing to do with any possible experience."

2. Kant offers a definite *solution* to the antinomies. He rejects the notion that the answer surpasses our capacity, that we must admit our ignorance, that the darkness is impenetrable. To his mind, the question must be "per-

fectly answerable," "because an answer must spring from the same sources as the question." Here we are dealing, not with a particular experience, but with experience of the world as a whole. Since the "thing" cannot be given in experience, "we must examine our idea itself to find out what it is."

The key to the solution of the antinomies is insight into the phenomenality of our existence in the world. Everything we experience is appearance, not thing in itself, not noumenon, but phenomenon.

The traditional speculations on the world as a whole were based on the theorem: "If the conditioned is given, the entire series of all its conditions is likewise *given*." Contrary to this, Kant says: "If the conditioned is given, a regress in the series of all its conditions is set us as a task." That is a "postulate of reason." The above principle of dogmatic speculation would be correct if the world were thing in itself and not phenomenon. But then the antinomies would be insoluble.

But if the world is appearance, the antinomies are soluble. The solutions fall into two groups. In the one, thesis and antithesis are both wrong, there is a third possibility; in the other, they are both correct, the thesis for the realm of the intelligible, the antithesis for the world of appearance.

The first group. If the world is being as such, the disjunction applies: It is either finite or infinite. But if the world is appearance, it is in itself neither finite nor infinite, but "only in the empirical regress of the series of appearances" and not "as something in itself." It is never wholly given; it is not an unconditional totality, but is always set us as a task.

Instead of hypostatizing the world as absolute being, we take the world as an Idea, a regulative principle guiding our progress indefinitely through experience. The Idea is not "a constitutive principle of reason, enabling us to extend our concept of the sensible world beyond all possible experience. It is rather a principle of the greatest possible continuation and extension of experience, allowing no empirical limit to hold as absolute. Thus it is a principle of reason which serves as a rule, postulating what we ought to do in the regress, but not anticipating what is present in the object as it is in itself, prior to all regress. Accordingly I entitle it a regulative principle of reason."

On the basis of his insight, Kant permits no statement concerning the world as a whole. We may not say: The world is finite, nor: The world is infinite, nor even: The regress is infinite, but only: The rule of progress in experience is that we should never presuppose an absolute limit. "The concept of the magnitude of the world is given only through the regress and not in a collective intuition prior to it."

The second group. The solution to the antithesis: there is freedom at the beginning of a causal sequence—everything is necessarily determined by causal laws, is that both are correct. In the world of appearances, unlimited causal necessity applies ad infinitum. For the consciousness of the ethical imperative, freedom applies in the sense that a chain of causality is started through me; but this awareness of personal freedom cannot become an object of empirical knowledge.

To Kant's mind the solution of the antinomies by way of transcendental idealism resembles a successful experiment. The direct proof of the phenomenality of the world in the "Transcendental Deduction" is confirmed by the indirect proof based on the antinomies.

The gist of the idea is: If the world is a self-subsisting totality, it is either finite or infinite. But according to the proofs of thesis and antithesis, both statements are false. Hence it is false that the world (the sum total of all phenomena) is a self-subsisting totality. The dogmatic proofs culminating in contradictions are not an imposture, but perfectly sound if it is assumed that phenomena are things in themselves. Or in other terms: The absolute cannot be conceived without contradictions. But if things are phenomena, in no sense unconditional, and if they draw their character from our manner of representing them, there ceases to be any contradiction.

3. Taking no fixed position, Kant penetrates all the contradictions of the antinomies; he gains mastery over all these conflicting ideas by perceiving their source.

The regressive and progressive series of experience are intuitive insofar as they take on sensuous content at every step. Absence of intuition, empty thinking whose propositions are necessarily contradictory, makes its appearance when the infinite, the unconditional, the totality is treated as an object.

The formulation of necessary antinomies and their solution by the distinction between the empirical and the supersensible is for Kant a means by which to confirm his fundamental insight in the course of his critical elucidation of ethics, aesthetics, philosophy of nature. Reason bares insoluble antitheses, which are solved by the insight that the world is not a self-contained system.

10. *The* Intellectus Archetypus

Perhaps our knowledge is not the only knowledge, but only one mode of knowledge. But since we know no other, the special characteristic of our knowledge, which is linked with the awareness of the phenomenality of our existence, can be gained only through a construction in which it is contrasted with another knowledge. Though we must always remain within our mode of knowledge and are unable to conceive of any other, we can attempt in this way to perceive the special nature of our knowledge. Kant does this in two ways. He sets up one construction that is less than our knowledge—a welter of intuitions: thereby the function of our knowledge to give lucidity is clarified—and another that is more than our knowledge, a divine intuitive knowledge, which clarifies the finite nature of ours.

The first: If every particular representation were entirely separate from every other, there could never be any knowledge: "Appearances might very well be so constituted that the understanding should not find them to be in accordance with the conditions of its unity. Everything might be in such confusion that, for instance, in the series of appearances nothing presented itself which might yield a rule of synthesis and so answer to the concept of cause and effect. This concept would then be altogether empty, null, and meaningless. But since intuition stands in no need whatsoever of the function of thought, appearances would none the less present objects to our intuition." Yet they would still be a mere jumble of experiences. "Without an object these would be nothing more than a blind play of representations, i.e., less than a dream," or a mere "rhapsody of perceptions that would not fit into any context according to rules of a completely interconnected consciousness."

And furthermore: without the unity of objectively experienced things, there would also be no unity of the self-consciousness. For "only insofar as I can grasp the manifold of the representations in one consciousness, do I call them one and all mine. For otherwise I should have as many-colored and diverse a self as I have representations of which I am conscious."

The ground of our lucid knowledge is the "transcendental ground of unity," which must lie both in me and in what affects me.

The second: Our knowledge is dependent on intuition. If we are to know, the spontaneity of our understanding must encounter the receptivity of sensibility. In regard to its form but not in regard to its existence, we produce the object we have before us and know.

At this point Kant conceives of intuitive understanding. It is not dependent on intuition. For in thinking it also supplies the intuition, the existence of the object it knows. To this understanding thinking and intuition are one. As creative understanding, it is the model (*intellectus archetypus*) in contradistinction to our reproductive understanding (*intellectus ectypus*), which is dependent on what is given to it. The archetypal understanding gives itself the manifold through its self-consciousness. Our reproductive understanding, the pure "I think," is totally empty, because it is dependent on the existence of objects. The supreme principle that all my representations are subject to the condition of the synthetic unity of the self-consciousness does not apply to the intuitive understanding. "An understanding which through its self-consciousness could supply to itself the manifold of intuition—an understanding, that is to say, through whose representation the object of the representation should at the same time exist —would not require, for the unity of consciousness, a special synthesis of the manifold."

The notion of such an archetypal understanding not only makes clear our dependence on intuition as a peculiarity of this finite faculty of knowledge. It also prevents us from attributing our forms of intuition (space and time) to all beings having a cognitive faculty. "For it may be that some beings in the universe can perceive the same objects in a different form; and it may also be that this form is the same and necessarily the same in all beings." But even if this is so, "we still do not understand this necessity, any more than we understand the possibility of a divine intellect which fully knows objects by mere [intellectual] intuition."

The reproductive, discursive, dividing and divided nature of our understanding compels us to differentiate understanding and sensory affection, the form and matter of our thought, the universal and the particular, possibility and reality, mechanism and teleology, and so on. We know only insofar as we separate factors which we can never fully bring together again but which can achieve their ultimate unity only in the supersensible Idea, that is, in pure being.

Accordingly, we can never apprehend the truth in its totality, because we can never apprehend pure being. Yet, for this same reason, what we apprehend is not untruth, but objectively valid existence as it appears in consequence of these separations. And because of the transcendental nature of our reason, this is the only way in which we, with our thought and intuition, can know things in general.

11. *Summary*

I shall try to sum up what has been discussed thus far.

Kant does not, like all earlier philosophers, investigate objects; what he inquires into is our knowledge of objects. He provides no doctrine of the metaphysical world, but a critique of the reason that aspires to know it. He gives no doctrine of being as something objectively known, but an elucidation of existence as the situation of our consciousness. Or, in his own words, he provides no "doctrine," but a "propaedeutics."

As we have seen, he examines the instrument of knowledge in order to see what it can accomplish, within what limits its judgments have validity. This examination is itself knowledge and, indeed, knowledge of an incomparable kind. Consequently the expression "instrument of knowledge" is ambiguous: in any case, this instrument must be examined not before it is used but while it is being used. It is not distinct from the matter it elaborates, but is the form of all conscious existence, that is, of what is elucidated in Kant's transcendental method. Philosophizing, said Jacobi at that time, is the elucidation of existence. Consciousness is an intelligible existence. The form of knowledge is present in every perception, in every mere object as such.

Science is the systematization of the knowledge that is everywhere present as existence. And transcendental philosophy is the self-understanding of this knowledge. But this is not enough.

The impression left by a first reading of the "Deduction of the Pure Concepts of the Understanding" and the related sections of the *Critique* ("The Schematism of the Pure Concepts of the Understanding" and the

"System of all the Principles of the Pure Understanding") is: Not a single demonstration is carried through step by step, from one decisive position to another. Rather, there is an interweaving, a circling and repetition which confuses the reader at first. We have attempted to show by our analysis that this is not carelessness but an expression of profound thinking. The involvement lies in the very nature of what Kant is elucidating.

Nearly everyone experiences at first an inner resistance in reading this central section of the *Critique,* but later on it is this section that arouses the greatest interest. It is here that we must look for the Kantian ideas that derive lucidity from the depths.

The remarkable thing is that Kant did not systematically ask what he himself was doing. He does not even employ the term "transcendental method," but speaks of "critical method" and transcendental philosophy. Hence the question arises: Can Kant's basic idea be systematically transposed from the tangled skein in which he embedded it into a clear development of distinct lines of thought?

Obviously, the uncommon intricacy of the ideas developed in and around the Transcendental Deduction is a sign that this is one of the nodal points of the Kantian philosophy. Several aims are so closely connected that they are attained at one stroke; but in our exposition they must be broken down and considered singly.

The aims are: To clarify objectivity as that whereby objects exist for us —to understand the cognitive faculty as the condition of all objectivity; to justify the claim of necessary and universally valid judgments; to understand that our knowledge is valid only within the limits of possible experience and that it is impossible to go beyond them; to derive the principles of all empirical science; to gain an awareness of the phenomenality of existence. In this last aim all the others converge. Two of them are of the greatest philosophical importance:

1) What we think in the categories has objective validity, but only within the limits of possible experience and no further. Metaphysics in the sense of objective knowledge of the supersensible or as ontology, which teaches being as whole, is impossible. Over against the congealed positions of the ontologies and cosmologies, Kant gains the flexibility of free investigation in the world. He secures the world as an infinite field lying open to experience. The world is not a closed system and cannot become one. Kant opens up this possibility of experience, but admits no objective knowledge that is not fulfilled in experience.

2) Kant's idea frees us from the natural faith in the self-subsistence of the world as the whole and exclusive reality, and frees us from confinement in our knowledge of existing things. He closes the door to the dogmatic empiricism that absolutizes the content of experience into pure being. While gaining insight into the possibility and validity of empirical knowledge, he recognizes its limits and carries the question beyond it. Philosophical

knowledge of the phenomenality of existence results in a consciousness of being which does not negate, but includes, the customary realism, yet goes beyond it.

IV. STRUCTURES OF REASON IN ALL ITS FORMS

What we know is not the world but only our ways in the world. Being is utterly inaccessible to our knowledge, but it has a manifestation in our existence, to which things appear and which appears to itself. Our understanding produces everything that appears and becomes object—in regard to its form. But it is a finite understanding, all reality must be given to it. It cannot produce the existence of a single grain of dust. Hence its knowledge is dependent on experience.

But from time immemorial the understanding has sought to penetrate to the ground of things by pure thought. It was encouraged in this endeavor by the supposition that if a proposition was free from contradiction, its content must be real. But though freedom from contradiction is a condition of objective knowledge, it is not sufficient to constitute objective knowledge. Ideas can be free from contradiction and yet relate to unreal, fantastic things. For freedom from contradiction applies only to the form, not to the content of knowledge. Hence metaphysical judgments are without foundation, because in them the categories are not realized in intuition. In such judgments logic (freedom from contradiction) is employed as a means of drawing from mere concepts conclusions about things that are inaccessible to experience. Where logic is employed not merely to ensure order in our thinking, but as an organ of actual knowledge, the great illusion arises. Here we have the "logic of illusion" that Kant calls dialectic. There is a "certain illusion" both in its positive and its negative statements.

This is what happened in connection with statements about the soul, the immortality of the soul, freedom, the world as a whole, God. Kant completely overturned the traditional metaphysics. Moses Mendelssohn in his fright said that he was crushing everything. But this is only the beginning of Kant's philosophy. Having explored the reliable knowledge of the understanding, he was not satisfied, but declared: "We are not satisfied with the exposition merely of that which is true, but likewise demand that account be taken of that which we desire to know."

Mathematics and empirical science yield solid ground, but it is limited in scope. "This domain is an island, enclosed by nature itself within unalterable limits. It is the land of truth—enchanting name!—surrounded by a wide and stormy ocean, the native home of illusion, where many a cloud bank and many a swiftly melting iceberg give the deceptive appearance of farther shores, deluding the adventurous seafarer ever anew with empty hopes, and engaging him in enterprises which he can never abandon and yet is unable to carry to completion."

Kant shows that the illusion of metaphysical knowledge lies in the nature of our cognitive faculty, and that once understood, the illusion still remains, though it no longer deceives us. Kant saw the deceptive mists clear away and the glittering icebergs melt, but in discerning the basis of the illusion, found a perverted form of a positive meaning. His decision to investigate this meaning as such opened up fertile new perspectives upon the supersensible ground of all things. Freed from its perversion, the truth of reason, which goes beyond the understanding and is destined to guide it, would become the central content of the Kantian philosophy. The elucidation of the structure, meaning, and limits of our knowledge is only the cornerstone and foundation.

Kant ventured out upon the stormy sea in search of the veritable treasure. He was far from the contemptuous indifference toward metaphysics that has characterized the positivistic Neo-Kantians.

How does Kant continue?

In order to become conscious of what we can know in the modes of thought through which being is for us, we must distinguish between our existence insofar as we know and those things that cannot be objects of our cognition. While in our existence our consciousness as such distinguishes one existent from another and we deal with contents, the total content of consciousness as such can be distinguished only from something that is not accessible to our understanding. We can think of it as a limiting concept, not as an object. After Kant has marked off the limits of our possible knowledge, there remains, outside them, what he calls the "thing in itself," the intelligible or noumenal world. Our understanding does not tell us whether it is or even whether it is possible. We can conceive of the boundary, but not pass beyond it. Whatever we may do, we as reality remain within existence, while as thought, we are confined to consciousness as such. We may suppose we have passed beyond them, but the next moment we are back where we started. By this method no advance is possible.

But what we cannot achieve with the understanding as something objectively known is accomplished by our reason. Kant discloses the faculties of reason: first in the efficacy of the Ideas (theoretical reason); second in ethical action (practical reason); third, in the contemplation of the beautiful (aesthetic judgment). After Kant's diagram of the structure of the understanding, we must now examine his more extensive diagram of reason. In our final summary, we shall examine the reality of the supersensible.

Here a methodological principle is introduced. As we have seen, what is conceived as a limiting concept cannot be known as an object. Or, as Kant put it: I can cogitate what I do not know. With this proposition he actually opened up the field that he seemed to have shut off completely. What we can think but not know is a vast field. This thinking extends from the play of the understanding at its limits to the elucidation of all the faculties of our actual reason. What is a futile adventure for the knowledge of the understanding becomes accessible through reason—in a different way, but never without the understanding. And this access opens up once the illusions of mere understanding are understood and dispersed.

A. THE IDEAS

Though the Ideas are without an object, they play a positive part in scientific knowledge, to which they first lend direction and meaning.

1. Negation of the Object of the Ideas

In the world I follow chains of causality back to the first cause or to the *world* as a self-contained whole. In investigating the subject of the *soul,* I proceed to the substance underlying all its phenomena, which preserves its personal identity while its states change. In considering each individual or the one total world, I conceive the total range of the possibilities of the existent, each particular of which pertains or does not pertain to this individual existent. In so conceiving the world, the soul, the whole of being, I suppose that I am dealing with an object. In each case, I acquire this object only by transposing categories that are valid for experience in my existence to infinities which, because they cannot be realized in intuition, elude experience. All objects are in the world, but the world is not an object. The soul is not an object, but becomes so only through the illusory application of categories of substance, duration, unity, to something which does not exist in experience. Total being (known as God) is not an object, for in conceiving the sum total of possibilities I have not conceived of something I might somewhere experience. Ideas manifest themselves where, in the progress of the knowledge of the understanding, I seek a conclusive whole; they mislead us if we suppose that the conclusive totality is a known object. They are never given, they are set us as a task.

All three Ideas—world, soul, God—foster a dialectical illusion which has given rise to the phantasms of metaphysics: rational cosmology, psychology, theology, an edifice without foundation. We treat the Ideas, which can never have an adequate object in experience, as objects and suppose that we know them. But this train of thought is a necessary illusion of our reason, not arbitrary sophistry. Critique can prevent the illusion from deceiving us, but cannot dispel it.

Kant took great pains in elaborating and expounding this negative result of his dialectic. But then he goes on: The Ideas of reason are dictated to us by our reason itself. It is not possible that reason includes fundamental illusions. Thus the Ideas must serve a purpose in our reason. They cannot, in themselves, be an illusion, but become one through natural misuse, through the perversion described above.

2. *The Positive Significance of the Ideas*

Empirical knowledge is infinite. The synthetic unity of individual experience formed by the categories creates the object, but it does not provide the systematic order of objects that constitutes a science. This we first acquire through the Idea, which provides representations of the whole.

Examples: we conceive the causality of a substance that is called force; we find many kinds of force; we attempt to reduce them to a few, and finally to a single fundamental force.

We see the manifold forms of plants and animals; we arrange them in species, genera, races, and try to reduce them to a single principle, a primary form from which they all derive.

We observe the manifold of psychological phenomena and order them on the basis of the Idea of a being which preserves its personal identity.

We see the world by following the conditions of events ad infinitum. But we introduce systematic order into our endless findings by the Idea of a whole world.

We conceive our total experience of all realities in a systematic order, through the Idea of a supreme ground of creative reason, from which all objects arise: God, for example, "as mathematician," as creator of reality.

In other words: soul, world, God, considered as delusions resulting from the dialectic illusion of our reason, are Ideas. We do not know them, but we make them into principles underlying the system of knowledge.

Through the Ideas we gain rules by which we advance our knowledge; but we do not arrive at the object of the Idea. The Ideas are therefore said to be regulative principles for the progress of science, not constitutive principles for the building of an object. The transcendent use of the Ideas is rejected as an illusion, while the immanent use of the Ideas is indispensable to the systematic character of scientific knowledge.

This does not prevent us from conceiving the Ideas as objects; actually it compels us to do so, but only analogically. They are represented as analogies to real things; not, however, as existing objects, but as the "schema of the Idea." This schema cannot be realized by any intuition, but only by the systematic progress of knowledge itself. The Ideas do not apply to an intuition which belongs to them, but to the understanding which, with its categories, forms intuition. The categories cannot shape the content of the Ideas into objects, but are employed in this connection only by way of analogy. This inherently false usage is indispensable as a schematism for our thinking which can operate only with objects. It is true when it is taken in this sense. It is misleading when it is misunderstood and taken as an attempt to know the object of the Idea.

In Kant the Ideas have three closely related functions. The first—*meth-odological*—function is the easiest to understand: here the Ideas are principles of systematic order, schemata, for the guidance of scientific progress, heuristic concepts (of this the principles discussed above provide an example). The second function may be termed *psychological:* here the Ideas operate as forces in the subject, as seeds striving to unfold. The third is the *objective* function: here the Ideas encompass something that rises from the source of all things. We shall examine the three functions more closely.

First, the *methodological* function: When we wish to ascertain what a class of animals has in common, we draw a schematic sketch, of "the" vertebrate for example. We do not ask whether or not the sketch is correct, whether or not such a thing, as the "original vertebrate" for example, ever really existed. We ask only: Is it useful? We wish to use it as a means of establishing what is present in every vertebrate and of formulating questions that will tend to advance our understanding of the vertebrate ad infinitum. The Ideas are perspectives that we apply to experience.

Second, the *psychological* function: We speak not only of the correctness but also of the importance of insights. The value of a truth can sometimes be determined, for example, by the practical use we make of it; or one insight may lead to another, so that the question is merely deferred from link to link ad infinitum. In all science the value of truth remains ultimately indeterminable. We say that an insight is profound or superficial, essential or nonessential, but we can never prove these evaluations. They relate to the meaning of science and they themselves are unscientific. In these value judgments the Ideas are at work. They are the hidden forces in scientific inquiry. Unconsciously every individual is guided by them and evaluates the depth or superficiality, the importance or unimportance of a scientific work according to the Ideas whose presence he feels in it, though he can never fully substantiate this judgment.

It is curious to note that though we strive for perfect clarity in science, we lose interest once we have achieved it. We desire clarity but clarity that is the expression of an Idea. The Idea is the obscure element in scientific achievement; it is the butt of criticism, but at the same time it is the condition of scientific productivity. What reason demands is not unclarity, but the Idea. It does not seek obscurity for its own sake but it is also not interested in mere correctness. The Idea perpetuates the problem and with it the unclarity. What is absolutely clear, and hence settled, is suspected of representing no Idea, of being merely correct and therefore pointless. Correct statements can be piled up ad infinitum; if they are to be of any interest, an Idea must connect them with a whole.

Third, the *objective* function: The things of experience give us something which, when successfully systematized and unified, corresponds to the Ideas. Consequently we may regard the Ideas as "consonant with nature." They "recommend themselves directly through their adequacy and not through any manipulations of method." Indeed, says Kant, reason could not logically "insist on deriving the manifold of forces from a fundamental force, if it were free to admit that all forces might just as well be incongruous and that the systematic unity of their derivation were not consonant with nature." Then reason would be setting itself a goal incompatible with the order of nature. Hence we must assume the systematic unity of nature to be objectively valid and necessary. Accordingly, Kant speaks of "the objective" though "indeterminate" validity of the Ideas, of their "objective reality," "but not in order to determine anything."

Thus Kant found something objective in the Ideas, and the central aim of his philosophy was to elucidate its nature. This is clearly borne out by his praise of Plato: "Plato was well aware that our faculty of knowledge feels a much higher need than merely to spell out experiences according to a synthetic unity, in order to be able to read them as experience. He knew that our reason naturally exalts itself to modes of knowledge which so far transcend the bounds of experience that no given empirical object can even coincide with them, but which must none the less be recognized as having their own reality, and which are by no means mere fictions of the brain."

If we look back over the three functions of the Idea, the psychological, methodological, and objective, we note that whenever we wish to grasp the essence of an Idea, we first approach it in one of the three functions. If we wish to apprehend it more fully, we pass on at once to the other functions, and the three become inseparable. In order to understand the one, we must understand all three. The Idea is at once subjective and objective.

Let us sum up what has thus far been said of Kant's *general view of knowledge*. The structure of knowledge begins with sensibility and its chaos of sensations, rises to space and time as the forms of intuition, thence to the categories which provide the objectively determined form of the intelligible, and, lastly, to the Ideas whereby knowledge progresses toward systematic unity. In this existence of knowledge, which in itself cannot be concluded but remains open, the supersensible makes itself felt by acts, not through any known content. In the phenomenality of existence, in this area of universal objectivity produced by the understanding, the Ideas are the breach through which the supersensible enters into knowledge.

Kant discloses this irruption of the supersensible in two highly important phenomena, our knowledge of living organisms and the role of theoretical ideas, which he investigates in detail under the head of "reflecting judgment."

3. *Life*

Living organisms are the existence of natural purposes. This statement calls for a clarification of the concept of purpose.

When I see something—such as a triangle drawn in the sand—which can only have been produced on purpose, I behold the trace of man. We distinguish such artifacts from products of nature, and when we find such traces, we conclude that men were present. For only in man, of all creatures in the world, do we encounter purposes and their realization through a will.

We regard the living organisms, the plants and animals, as natural reality. Organic beings are "things as purposes of nature." We conceive their purposiveness by a transference of our own purposive acts to the ground of their reality, and conclude that they are products of a purpose.

We conceive of purpose in nature in two ways: sandy soil is good (purposive) for fir trees, loam for grass and grain. In this way we judge the utility of things; this we do arbitrarily; what has just been treated as a purpose (grass) becomes a means (fodder), and so on indefinitely, because a final purpose can never be found. This purposiveness is an external aspect of the one-sided purpose-means relationship. It exists only for our individual thinking and is not an objective purposiveness. It is quite a different matter when a product of nature, such as the living organism, is considered as an objective purpose of nature. The organism is the objective being, in which everything is at once means and purpose; the whole is a complete cycle of purposiveness. We conceive of it not as an external, but as an inner purposiveness.

Let us consider the living organism more closely. "A thing exists as a natural purpose if it is in itself cause and effect." It produces itself: in respect to species by breeding, in respect to individuality by growth, in the case of injury by regeneration. Life builds itself up from the matter of its food with the help of substances that are its own product. An organic product of nature is an individual in which everything is alternately purpose and means. Nothing in it is gratuitous, nothing is without purpose.

Descartes saw the organism with its purposiveness as a machine. Leibniz formulated the radical difference between natural machines and those made by man: "Every organic body of a living creature is a kind of divine machine or natural automaton, which infinitely excels all artificial automata. For a machine constructed by human art is not a machine in all its parts. The machines of nature, however, i.e., the living bodies, are machines down to their smallest parts, ad infinitum. This is the difference between the divine art and ours." Kant holds to this distinction: Where the parts are ultimate parts, finite in number, and made of lifeless matter, we have a machine which, however complicated, can be conceived by the finite understanding and constructed from lifeless matter. It must be tended and repaired by man. A clock is a machine made from outside: it operates only in one direction and is not a self-contained totality of end and means that can take care of itself. If it is out of order, it must be repaired. But in the organism everything—in respect both to its form and its operation—is alternately cause and effect. Down to the smallest parts, it is alive. A machine has only motor force, the organism has creative force.

But Kant differs from Leibniz in one fundamental point. Kant does not say that the organism is an actual infinity of reciprocal end-means relations, but that we can investigate it ad infinitum, never arriving at an end. As far as we can determine, it resembles a machine; as far as our knowledge can penetrate, it is a machine produced by a divine understanding. Everywhere life makes use of the same causal connections that physics and chemistry investigate in inorganic matter. But nowhere are these causal connections life itself.

And so Kant says that we shall never see the Newton of the blade of grass, that is to say, a scientist able to fashion the most minute particle of life from lifeless matter, for to do so he would have to have become lord of infinity, instead of being merely, as in all construction of machines, master of a multiplicity that can be increased more and more but must always remain finite. He would have to effect the leap from the finite to the infinite, and for finite understanding this is impossible.

According to Kant, life is a fact and an Idea. This self-contradictory sentence means that without an Idea the fact cannot even be determined as such. The understanding with its categories does not grasp it but inevitably transposes it to the plane of facts, akin to the facts of inorganic nature.

Thus Kant rejects any objectivization of life as a whole—he denies that it can be broken down into known or theoretically knowable objects. The whole cannot be understood as a machine, although biological knowledge gives mechanical answers. Nor can the whole be grasped as an entelechy, vital force, natural factor, which would become the builder of the machine, although our mind must always conceive the living organism as though an architect and planner had built it. In investigating living things, we confront the infinite.

For Kant biological investigation has a special character: it finds relations of means and purpose; it asks how they operate and always supplies answers based on mechanical causality, or rather on physics and chemistry in the wider sense (not only on mechanics in the restricted sense). We cannot grasp the means-purpose relations as a whole, but we understand them insofar as we interpret the organism as a machine.

And yet the living organism stands before us as a whole. If we see it and do not doubt its existence, it is because the Idea makes us aware of the difference between the source of this reality and that of any reality which can be established by the understanding. That is why the humblest of living creatures, a worm or insect, inspires in us the awe that is unfailingly awakened by what surpasses the understanding, by what to the understanding is a miracle. But if we are forsaken by the Idea which first enables us to see this reality, we may amass a great store of knowledge concerning the mechanism of life and mistake it for life itself. But no more than the cow that we treat as a machine for the production of milk can we possess life with our knowledge. The awe is lost because we no longer perceive anything to arouse it.

4. Reflecting Judgment

The picture begun with the Ideas is completed by a train of thought disclosing the relation of all our knowledge to its source in being.

A. *The consonance of nature with our cognitive faculty; the existence of natural purposes:* The object constituted by the categories is exclusively an object of experience. It is recognized by the understanding as necessary, because it is determined by the conditions of all experience. It has objective priority; it alone is an empirical object that the understanding can apprehend through mechanical causality, or through mathematics in the widest sense. In the realm of this necessity there are no puzzles. But this realm itself calls our attention to its limits. What occurs at these limits is contrary to all necessity, that is, is *accidental*.

First example: In our experience, universal necessity is manifested through a multiplicity of special laws. But scientific knowledge is based on the assumption that, guided by the Ideas, we shall find a systematic relationship among these special laws. If, as is possible, there should prove to be so great a diversity of contents, rules, essences, that in comparing them the human understanding could find not the slightest similarity and could not, by reduction to principles, find the slightest relation among the particular laws, the Idea of systematic unity would not be confirmed. It would not be possible to amplify our experience by increasing the scope and unity of our knowledge; nothing would remain but an endless diversity of knowledge, an infinity of disintegration. There would be no science.

If knowledge is our purpose, it would be unattainable under these circumstances. If actually we progress, it means that nature serves the purposes of our cognitive faculty. We impute this purpose to nature as it were, because, in this connection, the understanding cannot prescribe laws as it does in the categories and principles governing all the objects of possible experience. We could make no purposive use of the Ideas, if nature did not itself possess purposive unity. There must be something in the ground of things that meets the Ideas halfway. There is a kind of communication between the demands of our finite understanding and the objective order of things in nature, but only insofar as nature complies with the demands of the understanding. For we cannot assume in advance a total coincidence between our cognitive faculty and the nature of things. Somewhere there might be a limit, where the Idea of unity would be disrupted and knowledge cease with it. Thanks to the Ideas, we expect the contrary, but we do not know. All we can say is that insofar as our systematic knowledge is successful, it points to a common ground of knowledge and of things.

Second example: The existence of living organisms—of things responding to purposes of nature—is a fact that the understanding with its a priori categories could not have conceived of. Never would the understanding, in examining things with its categories, suspect the existence of living creatures. If we consider nature according to the laws of necessary processes, all structures that seem purposive are contingent. Either they are produced by man; then their form stems from a causality which thinks purposively. Or else they are products of nature; then they are contingency, inexplicable on the basis of the mechanism of inorganic nature.

Both questions, the one arising from the consonance of nature with our cognitive faculty and the other springing from the existence of things as natural purposes, lead to the problem of contingency, or chance. Contingency means total indeterminateness, hence unintelligibility. Accordingly, our thinking cannot accept it. We examine it in the hope of subordinating it to a rule. The problem is: Do we find a law, a necessity of chance? Such a necessity would have to be radically different from that of the natural process.

Contingency is excluded from the natural process, whose laws make it accessible to our knowledge. That nothing happens through blind chance (*in mundo non datur casus*) is a principle of natural science. But every necessity is conditioned, hence comprehensible (*non datur fatum*).

There are undetermined or insufficiently determined events. Here too science seeks regularities—through statistics. In examining a large number of cases, it calculates the chances. Then it determines the probabilities in the individual instance and for the mass arrives at a law of large numbers. Kant's question, however, is concerned not with individual events or with masses of events, but with our knowledge as a whole. Here contingency cannot be overcome by any knowledge of the understanding that constitutes its objects. This contingency cannot be subsumed under any universal; it is the limit of the universal.

B. *Determining and reflecting judgment:* To explain the lawfulness of chance another approach is needed. This Kant develops through his distinction between determining (subsuming) judgment and reflecting judgment.

This distinction already plays a part in the theory of Ideas developed in the *Critique of Pure Reason* (here Kant speaks of the apodictic and hypothetical use of reason) and is further developed in the *Critique of Judgment:* Either we are in possession of the universal (the rule, the category, etc.) and subsume a case under it, or else we have the particular and consider it under the hypothesis of an unknown universal. Kant calls the first method determining, the second reflecting judgment. The determining judgment, which subsumes a particular case under the known universal, is within the grasp of reason. But the reflecting judgment, which first gives rise to hypotheses for systematic investigation, is beyond calculation.

The reflecting judgment is the intellectual operation that sees the particular in the light of a universal, which it does not know but by which it is guided. Always holding to the particular, never slipping into the abyss of the insensible and unintelligible, the reflecting judgment operates under the guidance of the Ideas. It provides principles of thought, but no new objects. The objects of the Ideas (mere schemata for our guidance) are conceived only in relation to advancing knowledge.

In Kant, the reflecting judgment has a wide scope. He sees it not only in the realm of cognition (in the Ideas rising from the consonance of nature with our cognitive faculty and in our knowledge of living things: in both cases, chance as purposiveness becomes necessary for the reflecting judgment); the reflecting judgment is also at work in the contemplation of the beautiful. The basic trait is the same: in the particular, the unknown universal; in the contingent, the lawful; in the empirical, an indication of something that comes out to it from the supersensible. The difference is that in the process of knowledge the reflecting judgment is only regulative and determines no object of its own, but that in the contemplation of the beautiful it is constitutive of the pleasure involved in judgments of taste.

c. *The area of contingency:* Not only the consonance of things with our cognitive faculty, not only the existence of the organisms are contingent. Contingency stands at the very threshold of our empirical knowledge: it is a matter of contingency that we have just these forms of intuition (space and time) and just these forms of judgment and categories.

As Kant states only briefly, but in no uncertain terms, the whole existence of things is contingent. Necessity means conditionality. Everything we know as nature is conditioned and thus determined. All our investigations in the realm of experience presuppose necessity. But the empirical world as a whole and the circumstances to which we have just referred are contingent.

This element of contingency raises the ultimate question in regard to the totality of being: Whence? and Whither? No answer is to be found that can disclose the necessity of being.

Unconditioned necessity, which we so indispensably require as the last bearer of all things, is for human reason the veritable abyss. . . . We cannot put aside, and yet also cannot endure the thought, that a being, which we represent to ourselves as supreme among all possible beings, should, as it were, say to itself: "I am from eternity to eternity, and outside me there is nothing save what is through my will, *but whence then am I?*" All support here fails us; and the *greatest* perfection, no less than the *least* perfection, is unsubstantial and baseless for the merely speculative reason, which makes not the least effort to retain either the one or the other, and feels indeed no loss in allowing them to vanish entirely.

In whatever direction we think, contingency remains ever present as the limit. When our knowledge degenerates into positing itself as absolute and supposes itself to be in possession of being, it veils this element of the contingent. It lies as an abyss before us. Every answer we give is dialectical, changing forthwith into a new question. But contingency is the signal which both warns and encourages us in our knowledge.

At this limit we seem to be faced with the alternative: either the total meaninglessness of the contingent or a necessary ground of all being, whence come direction and meaning. But Kant sees this alternative as another false question. For because the world and everything we know in the area of possible experience is appearance, a conclusive answer is not possible. We go our way in the world. When we try to apprehend the whole, the ground, the meaning, our thought, insofar as it becomes object, also belongs to the world of appearances. We cannot transcend this world by our knowledge of something, but solely by the course we take within it, by the experience of the Ideas in systematic knowledge, by the play of all our cognitive faculties in the intuition of the beautiful, and, truly and decisively, through our freedom in ethical action.

D. *The split in our knowledge elucidated by comparison with an* intellectus archetypus: Kant shows once again how our knowledge fails at this point, by contrasting our finite thinking with an *intellectus archetypus*. Previously the *intellectus archetypus* was considered as an intuitive understanding, which produces the objects it thinks, in contrast to our discursive understanding, which is dependent on intuition given it from outside. Here, however, the *intellectus archetypus* is considered as an understanding which unites such concepts as contingency and necessity, the universal and the particular, mechanism and teleology, which we can conceive only separately.

1. The ground of the distinction between possibility and reality lies in the nature of our cognitive faculty, which is split into understanding and sensibility. An intuitive understanding would have only real objects. It would contain no concepts disclosing mere possibility and no intuitions of anything we cannot know as an object. Our actual understanding can conceive of something that does not exist; and it can represent data without forming a concept. Thus the propositions: things can be possible without being real, reality cannot be inferred from possibility, are "correct for human reason." But they do not mean that the difference between possibility and reality lies in the things themselves. Our reason keeps telling us that there must be something (the primal ground) in which possibility and reality are indistinguishable, but at the same time our understanding has no concept whatever to fit such an idea. Necessity and chance, like all the other dichotomies, apply to our mode of knowledge, not to things in themselves.

2. Our understanding conceives the universal. However, it cannot derive the particular from the universal, but only subsume the particular under the universal when the particular is experienced. The particular is contingent. An intuitive understanding would pass from the universal to the particular without concepts; for it would be contingent.

3. Our understanding distinguishes mechanism and teleology. In accord-

ance with the special character of our understanding, we must consider the organisms as though, in regard to their possibility, they were created purposely, as aims. However, we do not assert that there is any such natural purpose or deny that "another (higher) understanding than that of man might find in the mechanism of nature the ground of possibility of such products of nature."

In each case we have the same situation: the *intellectus archetypus* contains in one what for us is divided, what we cannot in any way unite: intuition and thought; the universal and the particular; possibility and reality; mechanism and teleology. Our understanding inevitably gives rise to the dichotomies of our knowledge. Our reason sees through them, but cannot do away with them.

Thus the construction of the *intellectus archetypus* changes its significance according to the context in which it is employed. It is the intuitive understanding which intuits things and produces them in one: here the construction serves as a mere contrast to our mode of knowledge. The *intellectus archetypus* is also regulative reason, on the basis of which nature, in the course of our systematic progress, adapts itself to our cognitive faculties; and it is the ground of the unity between mechanism and teleology in the organisms. In both these cases the *intellectus archetypus* is not conceived merely as a contrast, but also as though it were the ground of the purposiveness of the contingent.

In this construction the fundamental insight is recapitulated: the difficulty lies not in things in themselves, not in being as such, but in the phenomena, the appearances. We know only the world of appearance; being is accessible to us only in the forms imposed on us by our cognitive faculty: this is the ever-recurring thesis, the meaning of which is merely enriched as we come to understand the structures, which are structures at once of our thinking and of appearances.

What we apprehend in our split thinking is not untruth, but neither is it the truth itself; we apprehend the reality of appearances, but not being as such. To say that we do not apprehend untruth means that, because of the properties of our reason, we must intuit and think as we do. This is how being is manifested to us; but the manifestation is objectively valid.

B. ETHICAL ACTION

1. The Categorical Imperative

Not only do we know objects; we also act. In acting, we choose. Here lies an ultimate source. Will, like knowledge, can be elucidated only in itself.

In our will we are aware of an ought, which is formulated in laws. Events follow the laws of nature with inexorable necessity. Actions should follow ethical laws but often do not. These laws are expressed in imperatives.

Imperatives are of two kinds. Hypothetical imperatives presuppose an end. If you wish to achieve the end, you must employ the appropriate means. Categorical imperatives on the other hand lay claim to universal validity. Hypothetical imperatives are technical; they are imperatives of dexterity and astuteness, guided by a superordinate aim; categorical imperatives have their ground in themselves.

A series of aims suggests the question: What is the ultimate aim? If the ultimate aim is a *summum bonum* (a material content), all imperatives are hypothetical. If there are categorical imperatives, the absolute must reside in the will itself. It can only be the form of the will, the law of its lawfulness. Kant's insight is: The good will is determined by a condition which is itself unconditional, discernible through pure reason, independent of all material aims in the world, a law that presupposes only itself.

This law is expressed in the one categorical imperative: "So act that the maxim of your will might always hold as a principle of universal law." Or: "Act as though the maxim of your action, through your will, were to become a universal law of nature."

"Maxim" signifies the subjective principle that I observe in my action. One set of maxims might be: I shall not accept a ride in a carriage that does not belong to me (because I should be deprived of my freedom); I rise at six in the morning (in order to have time for a good day's work). And another set: If I cease to love my wife, I shall get a divorce (because I wish to serve my happiness); if a great advantage is to be gained, I shall tell a lie; I regard contracts as valid only *rebus sic stantibus;* at the slightest change I shall feel justified in breaking my contract. Such maxims may be purely technical (first set). Or they may reflect a fundamental attitude (second set). In the first case, I test them by a theoretical knowledge of their effectiveness as means; in the second case, by the categorical imperative.

The central content of the categorical imperative is: "So act as always to treat man, both in your own person and in that of another, as an end and never solely as a means." For everything in the world, including man, can become a means of action. But every rational being who acts according to the categorical imperative—and the only rational being known to us is man—is also an end in himself; though under certain restrictive conditions he can be used as a means, he must never be used solely as a means.

The categorical imperative is a formal statement. To be applied in a situation, it requires "practical judgment." The rule of judgment is: "Ask yourself whether, if the act you have in mind were to take place in accordance with a law of nature, of which you yourself were a part, you could regard it as possible through your will." Kant speaks of "a man who honors the moral law and takes pleasure in imagining (as he can scarcely avoid doing) what world he, guided by practical reason, would create, if it were in his power." The meaning is: When you act, bear in mind that the world is not as it is, but that in your action you help to create it. It is not through knowledge but through your action that you learn what actually is.

2. *The Testing of Ethical Action*

Now the question arises: How, in a concrete situation, shall I test the maxim underlying my possible action? Through the understanding, I investigate the soundness of the law embodied in the maxim by the standard of freedom of contradiction. Certain actions—such as suicide—"are such that they cannot without contradiction even be conceived as a universal law of nature." The right to suicide would signify the negation of life itself. Other actions are such that in them the will contradicts itself. To embezzle a deposit would mean that there was no deposit; a lying statement would signify no statement.

When I have conceived the universal law, does the action, after scrutiny of the situation, follow by subsumption of the special case under the known universal law? No, for the material contents of our action—goods, aims, happiness—have different origins. But when I concern myself with these contents, a mere relative obligation gives rise to an absolute obligation through my consensus with an intelligible universal law. This consensus is the consensus of a rational being with himself and other rational beings.

The rational form of freedom from contradiction is only a reflection of the intelligible necessity of the law. When the law followed in the will is compared with the natural law, the natural law is merely "used to typify the law of freedom." Sensible nature is used as a model for intelligible nature.

Obligation and law are inseparable. An individual law would be a contradiction in terms or else the expression of a form of universal law that occurs only once. The obligation of law means that its necessity is recognized by the reason of a being who is a sensuous being.

I experience the unconditional demand by testing it in existence, where, in its pure formal character, it can be an unerring source of my action. It is not demonstrated by experience; but on the occasion of experience, it emerges in its inexorable, unerring power, which I can elude only by self-deception. It is not the imperative that confirms itself; rather, it is I who confirm myself through it.

As a sensuous being, I begin with habit, traditional customs, inclinations, and notions that I take for granted, without thinking. Then the Idea of reason strikes like a lightning flash, illumining what I did blindly and heedlessly. But for me as a sensuous being the Idea must gain its content in the reality of existence, through which it is first fulfilled.

Thus, the ethical law "borrows nothing whatsoever from experience," but applies a priori to rational beings. Yet, at the same time, the laws presuppose "an experienced faculty of judgment, partly in order to distinguish in what cases they apply, partly in order to impress them strongly enough on the will to ensure·their execution."

Kant found a new idiom for the ethical absolute. But in it he merely wished to express what every rational being unclearly knows and enacts. He speaks of the categorical imperative, which determines the law of our action, as the source that every man as a rational being recognizes. When we transgress against the law, we never actually wish to make the subjective maxim of our transgression into universal law. We only wish to make an exception in favor of our inclination.

3. *The Rise from the Psychological*

Let us once again examine the meaning of ethical freedom by rising up to it from the psychological phenomenon. Our faculty of desire is guided by impulses which limit one another. Into them enters our caprice which prefers and rejects in the medium of thought, and then seeks the means appropriate to the various aims it sets itself. This caprice is free in the negative sense; it is not bound by laws. It is mastered by the will, which is free in the positive sense, because it is its own law as reason.

Our morality is an ethical attitude in struggle. No man is endowed by nature with perfectly "pure sentiments." Kant calls it "sheer folly to flatter oneself into relying on an innate goodness of soul that requires neither spur nor check, nor even any commandment, and so to forget one's duty." Reliance on mere feeling for the right would be the end of human morality. Good inclinations, an upright heart, beauty of soul, are indeed most precious. But they must be sustained by lucid obligation. The tact and ethical sense of the subjective conscience provide a firm foundation only when they have risen from a pre-intelligible to an intelligible state.

Man as a finite being cannot be holy. Only for a perfect being can the ethical law be a law of holiness without conflict or struggle. For every finite rational being, it must be a law of duty. It is excellent to do good out of love of one's fellow men, or to be upright from love of order, but that is not enough. We also require the moral maxim of our behavior, which is appropriate to our situation as men, as rational beings among rational beings. Let us not say, with overweening pride, that we are above the concept of duty, or claim that we need merely do, uncommanded, for our own good pleasure, what requires no commandment.

It was in this light that Kant wrote the celebrated words: "Duty—word sublime and strong that implies nothing that pleases or charms, . . . nothing that threatens or inspires fear; your power is merely to establish a law before which all desires fall silent and which still is admitted to the chamber of the heart where it is held in reverence even if it is not obeyed. What origin is

there worthy of you and where may we find the root of your noble descent
. . . from which to be derived is the indispensable condition of a worth and
dignity that will owe nothing to anything or anybody but man himself?"

What is the root of this noble lineage? Kant says: It is what raises man
above himself (as a sensuous being), what attaches him to the order of
things that he can only arrive at by thought. Through this bond our sensuous
existence is subordinated to the pure being of the intelligible world. All
attempts to derive the moral law from something else have been futile.
Kant rejects the philosophical derivation from education (Montaigne), from
civil constitution (Mandeville), from inner perfection (the Stoics), from the
will of God as an outside force (theological moralists). In opposition to
all these principles implying a heteronomy, Kant posits the autonomy of the
human reason, "the idea of a rational being who obeys no law other than
that which he himself promulgates."

This law lies in the will itself; it is not given but produced, not read but
enacted. "The dignity of man consists in this capacity to legislate universally,
on condition that he obey his own legislation." The categorical imperative
does not come to man as a commandment from outside, which he must obey
because he is weak. No, man as a rational being gives himself the imperative,
it is his reason. Here reason is sustained by itself, but at the same time by
something more.

This is the source from which man derives his respect for his own law,
which inspires his reverence for that which transcends his senses and makes
him feel humble in the consciousness of his own dependence on his senses.

4. *Happiness*

Through this conception of an origin in which all ethics must be anchored
Kant upset the sovereignty of all notions of a material *summum bonum,*
earthly beatitude, happiness in the world. Once again he raises the question
that had been asked by so many philosophers: What is happiness?

"To be happy is necessarily the desire of every rational but finite being
and hence an indispensable determinant of his desires." Here Kant is in
agreement with all the moralists. Since every rational being wishes to be
happy, it is absurd to demand the will to happiness. It exists. But what is
happiness? The concept seems clear: Happiness is "the satisfaction of all
our inclinations" according to their diversity, degree, duration. It is "the
state of a rational being, whose whole existence fits in with his desires."
But it soon becomes clear that this definition defines an impossibility. Although everyone wishes to attain to happiness, no one "can say definitely
and consistently what he actually wishes." For this there are several reasons:

1. All elements of happiness must be experienced. Experience must teach
each man through his feelings of pleasure or pain wherein to situate his
happiness. Such experience differs from one man to another and in the

same man at different times, and it is never conclusive. Yet the "idea of happiness implies an absolute totality, a maximum of well-being in my present state and in every future state." The contradiction between the inconclusiveness of experience and the idea of perfect happiness in time cannot be overcome.

2. A maximum of happiness is an impossibility. For quantity of happiness cannot be evaluated.

3. It lies in the nature of "human desires that they can never be wholly satisfied." For inclinations change, they increase when favored and "always leave a void still greater than that one had planned to fill."

4. Happiness is not mere pleasure; it is only through reflection that pleasure and pain become happiness and unhappiness. We are happy or unhappy in accordance with conceptions we form of these two states. "Happiness and unhappiness are not sensations, but states based on mere reflection." A man "conceives of a desired state. This he does by his understanding which is involved with imagination and sensibility, in such different ways that nature could not derive from it a universally valid law that would correspond with so unstable a concept."

Consequently a finite being, even "one endowed with the greatest insight and ability," "cannot possibly form a definite concept of what he really wants."

From this insight it follows that happiness cannot be an end in itself. Ever since antiquity, this situation—the futility of desiring happiness when you have no way of knowing what you really want—had led thinkers to reflect on the meaninglessness of existence. Once attained, every state that has been identified with happiness brings disappointment. Is there nothing more? Our nature makes fools of us. Boundless desire drives us only to the experience of its absurdity. Kant does not deny the experience underlying these ideas. But in him the will that there should be a world is grounded in an idea that does not negate happiness but attaches it to something else. The infinitely manifold and unstable world of happiness, in itself without foundation or ultimate aim, is the medium of a realization which is subject to other conditions and other guidance than any form of material happiness considered as an absolute. Happiness and unhappiness derive their foundation and meaning from another order in which they are encompassed.

But our understanding does not penetrate to this order. Hence in our temporal existence there remains a cleavage: we strive for material happiness, but we subordinate our will to happiness to the condition of the categorical imperative. Kant does not reject happiness; far from despising it or looking upon it with indifference, he affirms it as a fulfillment. But in none of its stable forms can happiness in this world yield the ultimate measure. It is subordinated to the condition of the ethical imperative.

Yet the distribution of happiness in this world bears no relation to the distribution of ethical worth; no one can claim that only the good are happy and only the wicked are unhappy; we are forced to recognize that the reverse is also true. But Kant does not conclude that we should despair or abandon the quest for happiness. Instead, he finds in this state of affairs an intimation of the supersensible. The greatest good would be a perfect correspondence between happiness and ethical worth. It is embodied in the postulate of immortality which, unthinkable and indefinable, stands as a cipher of perfection.

5. Kant's "Formalism"

Kant's ethics has been criticized for formalism. The implication is that Kant does not tell us what we should do, that his categorical imperative is a mere formula. But this is Kant's express purpose. The question is only whether or not the formula is true and effective.

The same critics say that Kant disregards the material values, experience of which first makes ethical motives possible. The "material values" consist roughly (in ascending order) of: sensuous values (pleasant and unpleasant); vital values (noble and base); spiritual values (beautiful and ugly, right and wrong); and at the summit, holy and unholy. But to employ this sort of "ethics of material values" (Max Scheler) against Kant is to lose sight of the source and origin of Kantian thinking.

A. *Kant's doctrine of the form and matter of ethics:* Concrete action is filled with matter, the categorical imperative is formal. Concrete duty does not come from the form of the absolute, but from the world of appearances, from the will to happiness, from what appears to us as the highest good. The categorical imperative is empty if it does not fulfill its function as a standard of material action in the world. In a concrete situation the moral law must be clarified by technical knowledge and practical experience. But in the infinitely varied world of our action, the law alone can provide rational self-certainty—objectively, in respect to what is right, and subjectively in respect to the good will. Here lies absolute reliability.

B. *The origin of ethics:* Are not the great decisions like gifts that carry the actual content of all morality? Are formal questioning and formal confirmation not irrelevant at this point? Can I not betray the absolute, however I may have experienced it, in constellations where the categorical imperative does not even apply? Might it not be that the deepest guilt resides in areas inaccessible to any categorical imperative—where historical self-realization brings me to myself by bringing other men to themselves, where love is not merely ethical, juridical, practical, but is confirmed from a deeper source? Is there not a betrayal that has metaphysical reality though it cannot be grasped in terms of ethics? Is this deeper source not also the source of the material truth of the ethos that achieves self-clarity in the categorical imperative?

Even if this is so, the truth of the categorical imperative remains intact, indispensable, the source of all rationality, without which everything falls headlong into chaos and ruin. But no excessive claim is made on it; rather, it is preserved in its pure form as the symbol of a solid foundation rooted in the supersensible.

c. *The universal form and the historical content:* Many men tacitly assume that someone should tell them once and for all what is right and what they should do here and now in order to become good men and to contribute to the realization of a just order in the world.

Kantian philosophizing, where it moves consciously in the lucidity of its pure form, is a thorn that leaves us no rest along the way. Kant himself did not explicitly consider that verification along the way is a historical process that can never be brought to an end. Where he himself propounds a system of definite ethical principles, he discloses the historical form of his thinking, and moves away from the source. His concrete prescriptions tend to veil the pure form of the unconditional. There is a cleft between Kant's categorical imperative and his concrete ethical demands. The categorical imperative marks an eternal source; the concrete prescriptions are in good part an expression of the excellent, but historically contingent, ethics of eighteenth-century Germany.

D. *Principle, results, responsibility as a basis of ethics:* Criticism of Kant's "formalism" takes on a new depth with the question: What will be the consequences of an ethics which finds its absolute motive in pure principle as such, without concern for the results of an action, which sets up ethical laws and follows them regardless of the harm that may result? Man, according to this line of argument, is not good by virtue of his principles alone, but is responsible for the consequences of his action. The ethics of principle says: Do what is right and leave the consequences to God, or: *Fiat justitia, pereat mundus.* Those opposed to it can point to the evil that can be done in the name of moral principles. They can point to the violent men whose moral judgments have served their manifest desire to command and to torment other men. They can evoke preachers of morality who have been the basest of men because they have used morality as a weapon by which to achieve immoral prestige and power. Has Kant any bearing on this simplistic debate between principle and results as the foundation of ethics?

Extraordinarily drastic statements may be found in Kant. Ethical laws "command unconditionally, regardless of what the outcome may be; indeed, they demand that we leave the outcome wholly out of account, when a particular action is being considered." What need have men "to know the outcome of their moral commissions and omissions? It depends on the course of the world. For them it is enough that they do their duty." And Kant even wrote a short treatise demonstrating that it is impermissible to lie under any circumstances (*On the Supposed Right to Lie out of Love for*

Mankind). In hunting beasts of prey, he asks, am I justified in acting deceitfully, in luring them into traps to their detriment and my own profit? Kant would say yes, for animals are not rational beings. But what if another man, who is all-powerful, wishes to destroy me or those I love? What if he not only has total power but also lies, while I myself am utterly powerless?

Kant says that the system of the morality that is its own reward demands that everyone do what he should, but that the moral law is binding upon me even if others do not observe it. This applies to rational beings. But where all reciprocity has ceased, is there not a limit beyond which I am under no obligation to treat an individual as a rational being? Where men wield total terrorist power, or serve it or take advantage of it in their actions, am I not justified in treating them as wild beasts? Are deceit, dissimulation, even lies not only permissible in this case, but actually demanded by the categorical imperative? Are men to be regarded as human and rational beings simply because they belong to the human species and are capable of thinking rationally? Is the categorical imperative not blunted if, instead of speaking in its own right, it is translated into abstract injunctions such as: Never lie, or: Everyone who belongs biologically to the species "man" is a rational being and must be treated as such, even when to do so involves the risk or even the certainty that I myself or those I love will perish as a result.

The extreme limit, beyond which I am justified in no longer treating a man as a man, is attained only when he is in possession of unlimited power and uses it against me. But what if reciprocity vanishes to such an extent that only (or not even) juridical and no moral obligations prevail among rational beings? Where then is the limit? Do complete openness to reason, boundless patience, tireless striving for mutual understanding presuppose favorable situations and a consciousness of my own strength, without which they become a form of criminal self-destruction?

Ethical action cannot be considered separately from our material life in the world. Every concrete act has its consequences. The categorical imperative does not derive its unconditional validity from experience, but can fulfill it only by experience. The law can only be applied in view of the world. The consequences are a part of the material world in which the categorical imperative helps men to find the right way. To confuse the wonderful purity of this source of ethical reason with the rationalist rigor of definitely formulated commandments and prohibitions destroys the very source which Kant raised to consciousness. Kant has this source in mind when—perhaps mistakenly—he speaks of particular and definite ethical laws.

Consequently, the opposition between principle and results as a basis of ethics is not tenable. The ethics of principle itself demands that in concrete action guided by the categorical imperative, one should bear the consequences in mind. The true basis of ethics is a third factor which Kant, who obviously has it in view, does not expressly mention but which Max Weber brings out clearly in his "ethics of responsibility." Ethics of responsibility is the true ethics of principle. It does not take mere results or rational principle as its guide but seeks its way in the open area of possibility, pursuing an absolute that is not manifested through any material content, but only through thought in action.

6. Freedom

Ethical action *presupposes freedom*. Does freedom exist?

The investigation of nature and of all reality teaches us that there is no freedom. For things are intelligible only insofar as they are subject to the necessity of a natural law. Hence all cognition confirms the theory that freedom is nonexistent.

But the presence of an ethical "ought" teaches us that freedom does exist. I cannot elude the inner voice that tells me what is right and what is wrong. The categorical imperative expresses the principle of this insight of reason into itself. The "ought" implies a "can." Hence there is freedom.

My knowledge of the inevitable course of things in nature and my consciousness of responsibility seem to be mutually exclusive. Either nature has no inexorable chain of causality and is interrupted by acts of freedom, or else responsibility is a fallacy, freedom an illusion. If it is an illusion, it can only be investigated as a psychological phenomenon within the lawfulness of nature. This old question—the inability of natural science to justify man's consciousness of freedom—moved Kant deeply.

He found a solution in the phenomenal character of our existence. The categories as principles (e.g., the causal necessity of all happening) have objective significance throughout the realm of possible experience. Apart from them I can have no objective knowledge. But my awareness that all objects of my knowledge are appearance is rooted in a limiting concept which itself relates to no object—the thing in itself, the noumenon, the intelligible. And this thing that cannot be known is present in our freedom. For, indeed, there is no freedom if I look for it objectively, psychologically, or as a process that can be investigated. So far as investigation extends, there is no freedom. Freedom is not an object of cognition; it becomes reality through my action.

This is the simple relationship brought out by the network of concepts with which Kant explores the question of freedom. They raise it more clearly to consciousness. Let us now examine a few examples of his reasoning.

A. *The solution of the antinomy of necessity and freedom:* We have spoken of the antinomy: every cause has other causes ad infinitum, and all things are subject to causal necessity. On the other hand, the series begins with a first cause; that is to say, there is freedom. The first proposition applies to the investigation of the world of experience. The second, however, is not meaningful as a thesis concerning the beginning of the chain of natural causality, but cuts across it.

Because in our action we are subject to an "ought," we presuppose a first cause in considering the possibility of action. The first cause is not "subject to temporal conditions." Free actions have no temporal origin, but a timeless origin in reason. What is eternal is decided in the temporal phenomenon. Where what is is subject to no temporal conditions, "nothing happens," there is "no change," nothing begins. It is only in the world of appearance that what in the thing itself has no beginning begins. But how are freedom and phenomenal existence to be reconciled? What is their relation to one another? Our thinking becomes caught in contradictions, because the intelligible ground of phenomena (which in this case we ourselves are) cannot be conceived objectively and consequently, in our thinking, provokes the logical discrepancy we have discussed above. On this question a few brief pointers must take the place of an analysis:

The theory of two causalities offers a rationally simple solution, but at the cost of involving a second objective world. The theory runs: The proposition that every effect in the world must arise either from nature or from freedom does not present a true alternative. Actually, "both can be true of one and the same event seen in different aspects." In respect to its intelligible cause, an action may be regarded as free and, in respect to appearances, as necessitated by the course of nature.

The problem takes a different turn when we consider the effect of the intelligible upon phenomena. Freedom begins a chain of causality in the phenomenon, but in the sense that the phenomenon which results from former states through natural causality is produced from the intelligible by the causality of freedom. This effect of the atemporal on the temporal means that in the intelligible itself there is no freedom but the necessity of reason. Freedom first occurs in the relation of the timeless intelligible to the temporal phenomenon. "Between nature and the intelligible a third term: freedom." Neither does nature have freedom, nor "can we find an appropriate concept of freedom for pure creatures of the understanding, for God, for example, insofar as His action is immanent."

This is in keeping with Kant's idea that only caprice, not the will, is free. "The will that is oriented toward nothing other than the law can be called neither free nor unfree." Freedom, then, lies only in the caprice that can decide rightly or wrongly, not in the intelligible freedom of the will, for which there is no choice, because it belongs eternally to the necessary laws of duty. Freedom can never be seen in the fact that a rational subject can also make a choice that is in conflict with his (legislative) reason. "The capacity of deviating from this inner legislation is actually an incapacity."

Kant calls the source that is itself timeless the "intelligible character." It is the "cause of my actions as phenomena," but it is not itself a phenomenon;

it is not conditioned by causality, but free. In Kant's view, however, the empirical character fits the intelligible character. Here Kant suddenly begins to speak, not of the noumenon, the undetermined limiting concept, as the source of freedom, but of a multiplicity of intelligible characters—but only provisionally, for here we have the germ of an un-Kantian metaphysic. Schopenhauer pounced on this point, saying that we perceive in our actions with horror or delight what we ourselves eternally are and what we can no longer change. Actually this is not Kant's thought at all. In his eyes, quite on the contrary, every rational being is capable at any moment of starting all over again, despite the chain of previous states with their overwhelming causal determination. My eternal being may at any time turn out to be quite different from what it has hitherto seemed. And is it being in the first place? *This* being has in Kant a completely different meaning from the empiric being of the phenomenon.

But ultimately Kant states that our understanding is quite incapable of conceiving in one two things that for him are radically separate: intelligible freedom and phenomenal necessity. This could be done only by the *intellectus archetypus,* the intuitive divine understanding. This is what makes possible the paradox that one and the same thing is causally determined in the world of phenomena and free as an intelligible act. Such paradoxes arise because we always become involved in contradiction when, in our thinking, we pass beyond the objectively thinkable. In accordance with this same contradiction, we explain "past free actions according to the laws of human nature, but we do not recognize that they are determined by it, for if we did, we should not be able to say that they should have been different."

I cannot know that there is freedom; if I could, I should neglect to fulfill it by action. Nor can I know that there is no freedom; if I thought so, I should, by denying freedom, lose it. The thinking which apprehends by questioning and then continues to question what has been apprehended is the form of the philosophical investigation of freedom.

B. *Freedom is not an object of experience:* Can we "experience" freedom? Do we ascertain it through a mode of experience? If there is experience in this connection, it is only the experience of the "ought"—we hear the voice of reason in the categorical imperative. But Kant calls this experience only a "semblance of a fact." Freedom itself cannot be experienced but only presupposed. The concept of freedom "is transcendent for theoretical philosophy," because "no appropriate example of it can be given in experience." But Kant gains certainty of the reality of freedom through the practical principles underlying our use of it. The "ought" presupposes a "can." If ethical demands are to have meaning, man must have the freedom to fulfill them. In recognizing the law, I attain certainty about the premise on which it is based. But this does not mean that freedom is demonstrated by theoretical experience. "For if reason is practical, it demonstrates its reality and that of its concepts by action, and all hairsplitting against the possibility of its being so is vain."

In the inner sense we have psychological intuition of ourselves. Here again freedom does not enter. What I observe as my experience is appearance. The fact that we have no intuition of what we in ourselves are—as freedom—makes investigation of it impossible. It is impossible because man, "in view of what in him may be pure activity (of what does not arise through affection of the sense but comes immediately to consciousness), must consider himself as belonging to the intellectual world, of which he can have no further knowledge."

The category of causality, if we have in mind the causality of freedom, cannot be filled in by intuition but only by action. But this action is not accessible to intuitive knowledge, because it is not subject to temporal conditions. Kant's reflection teaches us to gain earnest awareness of ourselves. It leads us to the boundary between temporal existence and timeless being, but permits us to cross it only by ethical practice.

c. *Only by insight into the phenomenality of all existence accessible to our knowledge can freedom be saved:* For Kant only the doctrine of the phenomenality of objective existence stands in the way of any denial of freedom. "If phenomena are things in themselves, freedom cannot be saved." For then "nature is the complete cause of every event." The elimination of "transcendental freedom" as conceived in the distinction between being as such and appearance (by which the antinomy was resolved) would "at the same time eradicate all practical freedom." We do not gain immediate awareness of freedom through the inner sense; it is demonstrated by the concept of duty. Through duty and freedom man gains awareness of himself, "not as he appears but as he intrinsically is." Freedom is the point where the supersensible is present in this world, where we can, as it were, grasp it in our hands though we can never know it as a something in the world. This is "the glorious disclosure that comes to us from practical reason through the ethical law, namely the disclosure of an intelligible world." Only the concept of freedom makes it unnecessary for us to look outside ourselves for the unconditioned and supersensible substrate of the conditioned and sensible. For through the unconditioned practical law, our own reason knows itself to belong to the supersensible world.

In our understanding of Kant's conception of freedom, we may take two fundamentally different attitudes: either we may, with Kant, transcend all objectivity to attain self-awareness through a consciousness of being, grounded in freedom; or else we may assert a being in itself, an inherent objectivity and reality, and through such thinking lose our freedom.

d. *False explanations of freedom:* Instead of maintaining Kant's ideas on the plane of transcending philosophy with its paradoxes and contradictions, we may try to make things easier for ourselves by contenting ourselves with apparent explanations of freedom, based on immanent knowledge. But intellectual honesty forbids us to talk our way out of the indispensable contradictions with the help of such notions as the following:

1. Freedom is made possible by gaps in natural causality. The notion is false, for there are no gaps in the laws of nature which we can investigate ever more deeply without ever completing our knowledge of them. They apply to all phenomena accessible to our knowledge. But it is a' mistake to absolutize the hypothesis (which is perpetually confirmed by our cognition) that everything knowable without exception is subject to natural laws and assert that all reality is nature and hence knowable. On the contrary, the basic fact is that we, through our existence as knowing and acting rational beings, are something more than any data of our cognition. Our reality can never become an object of psychological or scientific knowledge, though as phenomena we are open to psychological investigation ad infinitum.

2. Freedom is a natural process of a special kind. Contingency and caprice are an unpredictable element in the natural process. From Epicurus, who drew a connection between free will and the accidental deviation of the atoms from their rectilinear course, down to the modern identification of freedom with unpredictable leaps in the atomic process, which can be apprehended only statistically, men have found satisfaction in saving freedom by objective means. But all this has nothing to do with freedom. Contingency or caprice as a limit to our knowledge of nature has no bearing on freedom, but is merely an element in our phenomenal world. Here again freedom is lost by being attached to an object.

3. In this view, the supersensible is, on the one hand, an infinity of individual intelligible characters of freedom and, on the other hand, a mere universal obedience to the one valid law of reason. In both cases, freedom is lost. In the first it is replaced by a multiple and thinglike supersensible; in the second by spurious "validity."

4. Nor can I grasp the meaning of freedom by reaching out into the future, plotting and planning it as though it could give me possession of eternity; nor again, by looking back into the past and conceiving it as the enduring, eternal reality. In neither case is time transcended in favor of freedom; on the contrary, freedom is taken back again into a falsely absolutized time. Real freedom cuts across the totality of time, which in the present unites past and future.

E. *The many dimensions of freedom:* Kant's philosophy of freedom unfolds like spokes radiating from a center. In speaking of "transcendental freedom," Kant discloses the center as a mere possibility; he shows that freedom can be conceived without contradiction, and so opens up an area in which the flame of freedom can be kindled. This freedom shines, as it were, in different dimensions:

Freedom is already present in the spontaneity of the understanding:

"Actually freedom is only the spontaneous activity of which we ourselves are conscious. The words 'I think' already indicate that even in my representations, I am not passive, but a free agent." Accordingly, the "self-consciousness a priori" is termed freedom.

Although the understanding is spontaneous, it is nevertheless bound to sensible representations. Reason, however, in the Ideas, shows so pure a spontaneity that it goes beyond everything sensibility can provide. With its power to distinguish between the sensible and intelligible worlds, it "prescribes limits even to the understanding."

Freedom has its decisive place in ethical action, in practical choice guided by the ought.

And finally, in the "free play" of our contemplation of the beautiful, freedom anticipates perfection.

c. CONTEMPLATION OF THE BEAUTIFUL

Contemplation of the beautiful, or, as Kant calls it, the "judgment of taste," moves men and gives them a pleasure which becomes deeper and more intense the longer they dwell on its object.

1. Judgment of Taste and Logical Judgment

Compared with logical judgments, a judgment of taste is always individual, never universal. Its predicate is not a concept, but a feeling of pleasure or pain. We cannot predict it but must experience it for ourselves. When someone tries to demonstrate why a poem, a painting, is beautiful, "I stop my ears."

The judgment of taste has "no interest" in the reality of the object. In this it differs from the enjoyment of the pleasant and the approval of the good. Independently of the sensory stimulus and of ethical satisfaction, the judgment of taste takes its object only as an occasion for a free movement of pleasure.

But this object is regarded as an object of universal pleasure. Everyone is expected to experience its beauty as valid, but there is no universal rule it can be said to exemplify. It embodies a "lawfulness without law," that can be experienced only in an individual judgment, that is, in a judgment of individual taste. This universal validity is therefore fundamentally different from that of a logical judgment.

In beholding a beautiful object, we form an idea of purposiveness but not of any particular purpose. If the perfection of an object is seen in its fitness for a purpose, such perfection is not beauty. Beauty is not an obscurely and confusedly perceived perfection. In beauty we behold a radiant truth, but not the knowledge of any object.

2. *The Free Play of the Cognitive Faculties*

Kant asks what the universal validity of a pleasure means. It is a free play of all the cognitive faculties, of imagination and understanding. Its harmony springs from a concordance of the cognitive faculties, in which no definite concept restricts the imagination to a rule of cognition and yet the imagination is not without a rule. It is the unity of freedom and law.

This freedom is distinguished from ethical freedom and the freedom of theoretical speculation. Whereas these two relate to a determinate and real causality, the freedom of aesthetic play is the most perfect, because it is unconfined by interest and reality. In its infiniteness, it is the actuality of all being. The inexhaustible ground can be felt in this tangible object. It is lost if a definite, formulable law—for example a mathematical law, be it ever so intricate—guides the play of contemplation. The essence of this freedom is an indeterminate and indeterminable, an infinite harmony.

3. *The Validity of Judgments of Taste*

A judgment of taste can have validity for all men only if all men as rational and sensuous beings have something in common. Kant calls this common element the "common sense." It is an "effect resulting from the free play of our cognitive powers," "the accordance of the cognitive powers to form a cognition as such."

4. *The Supersensible in Judgments of Taste*

Kant stresses the uncertainty of correct subsumption in judgments of taste. Here, where derivation ceases, where the feeling of pleasure is the only predicate of judgment, a new and fundamental responsibility arises: to perceive the supersensible through participation in the universally valid.

The judgment of taste is not a mere incidental faculty (like that of the wine taster) but contains the actuality of our whole essence. For it operates in the harmony of all the faculties of our reason. As the mere form of play, it is without essential material content, but in the tangible sensuous phenomenon the form itself is the content.

Free play in judgments of taste gives me as a sensuous and rational being awareness of the area in which everything that is being for me is situated (the play of all the cognitive faculties); therein it makes me aware of the unknown root of the two stems (sensibility and understanding), and through it leads me to something still deeper: The determining ground of the judgment of taste lies "perhaps in the concept of that which can be regarded as the supersensible substrate of humanity." For "in the supersensible lies the point of convergence of all our a priori faculties." Hence the philosophical insight that in the judgment of taste "no rule or prescription, but only that which cannot be subsumed under rules and concepts, i.e. the supersensible substrate of all our faculties, serves as a subjective standard."

5. *The Aesthetic Idea*

This standard in the form of the sensuous presence of the beautiful Kant calls the "aesthetic Idea." It is a representation of the imagination in its free play and cannot be captured by any concepts. Kant gives the name of Ideas to representations which relate to an object but which can never become a knowledge of it. A theoretical Idea can never become a cognition because it contains a concept (of the supersensible), to which no intuition can ever correspond. An aesthetic Idea cannot become a cognition because it is an intuition to which no concept can be adequate.

6. *Genius*

When Kant speaks of the beautiful, he does not at first distinguish between nature and art. But then he perceives the great difference: The contemplation of the beautiful is either free contemplation of an object, or else it is the creative play which brings forth the beautiful in art and poetry. Art and poetry create objects that make the beautiful communicable.

The creator of such works is called a genius. Kant limits the concept of genius to these creative men. Genius produces something that becomes materially present for intuition, the object, to which no concept can be adequate, which makes possible the infinite play of our imaginative powers. Genius is a gift of nature, through which nature, in the work, gives the rule which is indefinable, inimitable, and unrepeatable. It is nature in reason, insofar as it anticipates in play the perfection of phenomenal reality.

Genius is original. But since there is also original nonsense, it is more significantly the faculty of bringing forth a rule: it is exemplary. The nature of genius is the unity of all the faculties of the mind in creative production; it is the faculty of representing aesthetic Ideas. This nature is itself "the supersensible substrate," "and to make all our cognitive faculties act in harmony with it is the ultimate purpose, dictated by the intelligible in our nature." In a posthumous notation Kant wrote: "We should not say: geniuses. Genius is the unity of the world soul."

Genius remains an ambiguous concept in Kant. On the one hand, it is an origin, a power in its own right, it creates form. On the other, it is matter, it must be cut to shape and polished. On the one hand, it derives the standard from the supersensible substrate; on the other, its work is guided by "taste." Nature communicates the rule through genius ("where spirit shines forth, we are safe from all error"); and then again, taste regains its priority. Genius is nature, that is, the unity, in the supersensible substrate, of all the faculties of the mind (imagination, understanding, spirit, taste); but elsewhere it is matter on which form must be imposed by schooling.

7. *Unity of Nature and Freedom*

Kant finds in genius the unity of nature and freedom which are so radically separate in ethics. But this unity exists only in the realm of play, which is without moral obligation but acquires an obligation of its own through the rule and the Idea, which are fulfilled ad infinitum in the work of art. If nature were taken as the life of our psycho-physical existence, freedom would be "naturalized" and so lost. But here we have a nature that gives art its rule; this nature is our supersensible essence, and art (play) is the only language in which the whole of it finds expression.

8. *Limitation of the Concept of Genius*

Kant refuses to universalize the concept of genius. The scientist with his wealth of insight and his power of systematization, the statesman with his ethical gift, the technical inventor—each has his peculiar greatness. But Kant would not call any of these a "genius," nor would he speak of "genius of the heart." Only in connection with the scientist did Kant explicitly define this distinction, which lies in the character of the product. A genius is essentially different from a "great mind." The latter discovers "what might have been learned" and can be learned after him. Kant sees an essential difference between a work which, once created, can be studied and understood down to its very roots, and a work which provides endless food for thought and is as inexhaustible as the world itself. The steps of scientific progress can be repeated identically. A work of art cannot be repeated, it is always unique and complete. Scientists and poets have an essentially different gift.

Kant distinguishes just as sharply between aesthetic play and ethically binding action in the world. Every man should be moral, but not every man can or need be a genius; the concept of genius enables us, regardless of the morality of the artist, to understand his art, which is the free play of his whole being, hence always individual and irreplaceable.

9. *Beauty and Ethics*

In the free play of art and poetry, the source of the whole man is actualized. But this free play carries no moral obligation. Play is an infinite liberation, but not in terms of reality. It is by this liberation—from enjoyment or morality or logically determined knowledge, which all confine man to a particular reality—that he gains his magnificent liberality. But here there is an ambiguity.

In one connection Kant maintains that there is no relation between taste and morality: virtuosi of taste, he writes, are "ordinarily vain, stubborn, and given to disastrous passions." And in another: "The true propaedeutic for the establishment of taste" is "the development of ethical Ideas and the cultivation of ethical feeling."

Kant's insight in these matters culminates in the discussion of the ethical significance of the beautiful: Natural beauty is reality. Even though, in Kant's view, interest in the beauty of art is no proof of attachment to morality, a spontaneous interest in the beauty of nature is "always the hallmark of a good soul." But this is based on "interest" in the reality of natural beauty as a symbol of the supersensible source.

But, in the end, the proposition that "the beautiful is a symbol of morality" covers also artistic beauty. The exemplary creations of genius are irreplaceable. For art develops liberality of mind, a spirit of community is inculcated through the communicability of beautiful form, and by making us aware of the supersensible substrate, art makes us receptive to ethical ideas.

D. KANT'S PHILOSOPHICAL ELUCIDATION
OF THE SUPERSENSIBLE

Our thinking has its foundation, starting point, and medium in the understanding. In summing up, let us try to characterize the thinking of the understanding.

It is dependent on sensible intuition. In its representations space comes first, while time is intuited indirectly, by a line in space, for example. The objects of this thinking enter into an external relationship, after the manner of points in space. For the understanding, the parts are separate elements of a structure that sums up the whole. They attract or repel one another like bodies in space. Change comes about through a regrouping of the elements, or else it is motion in space.

In order to think, the understanding requires at least two points of reference. What it thinks is a relationship, in judgment, between two points or spheres: subject and predicate. The forms of judgment are regroupings of thought content; these may be visualized as spheres in space. The appropriate form of the relations is defined in syllogistic thinking. In the concepts, the understanding thinks classes, definable identities, subsumptions of the more particular under the more general. Things are instances which may be subsumed and interchanged. The individual is inaccessible to the understanding.

The understanding operates according to a linear end-means relationship: to attain this end I must apply this means.

The appropriate object of the understanding is inorganic matter, mechanical causality. The understanding apprehends the machine, not life. The inwardness of the soul and the movement of the spirit elude it. When it attempts to think them, it denatures them according to its own forms, in which they wither away. It can think them only in relationships that have no bearing on their essence.

But here is the remarkable fact: This thinking of the understanding is indispensable; it is the condition of all determinateness and clarity. But the world that corresponds to it is the colorless and barren realm of the machine, the movement of the elements and their combinations, mechanical causality, fabrication, contingency. From time immemorial man has utilized the thinking of the understanding and transcended it. The pure elaboration of the understanding brings clarity without content, and if mere understanding tries to transcend itself, the result is unclarity of content. Both its distinctions and its combinations harbor delusions. The clarity of the understanding operates within clearly defined, comprehensible limits. To abandon the understanding is to succumb to vain dreaming. Kant's philosophizing is a new form of philosophical thinking which with the understanding goes beyond the understanding but without ever losing it.

Thus Kant showed that even the knowledge of the understanding, when in systematic investigation it becomes science, is guided by the Ideas. He showed that the fact of life itself is inaccessible to the understanding. In the freedom of ethical action, he designated a reality springing from another source and disclosed the reality that is actualized in the contemplation of the beautiful, the play of the cognitive faculties.

This transcending of the understanding with the understanding does not permit any isolated faculty to operate without the understanding. But from other sources the understanding derives functions it could not derive from itself alone. The transcending of the understanding takes the form of the "reflecting judgment," which legislates for itself but never defines an object. Its movement implies the divine intuitive understanding, the divine teleological understanding, the union of all our faculties in the supersensible substrate of mankind, our intelligible being as freedom—but all this indirectly; they never become objects. Of this transcending of the understanding, Kant says: The transition is not "to another thing, but to another way of using reason." In each case, there is a leap: from correct knowledge to essential truth, from action that is technically correct to ethical action, from the correct judgment of taste to the aesthetic Idea—in each case from a conditioned to the unconditioned, from finite to infinite, from the endless to the meaningful, self-contained whole.

This going beyond the understanding does not mean that there are two worlds between which we might shuttle back and forth, losing the one when we are in the other. Rather, there is only the one reason, which goes astray unless, in one simultaneous operation, it holds together what it cuts apart. The universe in which we live is one. In Kant truth is only in the totality.

1. *Rational Faith*

In cognition, in the contemplation of the beautiful, and decisively in ethical action, reason incurs the need to complete itself. Cognition culminates in the Idea, an "as if"; the contemplation of the beautiful ends in the "play of the cognitive powers" and ethical action in the question of the meaning of what I do. In each case, the supersensible is present, but not for our demonstrative knowledge. The only principle by which we attain to certainty through reason is the striving of reason itself for "completeness." Reason itself has its ground in the rational faith it creates. Reason attains, by thinking, to its own presupposition, which is an indispensable part of its own completeness.

At the center of reason's need for completeness stands the ethical. Ethical action would indeed be subject to the same norms and have its own dignity even if there were no God and no immortality, but it would have no meaning in the universe as a whole. It would be without ground and aim, without faith and hope. Hence ethical action gives rise to the "postulates" that God is and that the soul is immortal (the "postulates of practical reason").

In the postulates we have a metaphysics rooted in practice; but they cannot be a cogent theoretical knowledge logically deduced from practice. They are only a meaning of which we gain awareness in the course of our ethical action and which we express in the theoretical medium, as postulates. "The ground for believing them to be true is here purely subjective, namely a compelling need of reason to presuppose, not to prove, the existence of a supreme being."

"Every use of reason that does not accord with the principles of experience is delusion, e.g., to suppose that one feels celestial influences, that one exerts an influence on the realm of spirits." But: "Although it cannot be achieved, ethical perfection is not a delusion. . . . God is not a delusion."

A belief involving a theoretical judgment is termed doctrinal belief: for example, the belief that God must exist, because without the presupposition of God there could not be a purposive order of things, that is, things as natural purposes (organisms). But doctrinal belief is "insecure." To say that the Ideas have "objective significance" can never mean that their content is objectively known, but only that they are valid in the systematic progress of knowledge. For Kant ethical faith is a different matter. I am certain, he writes, "that nothing can shake this faith, for if it were shaken, my ethical principles themselves would be shattered." Hence we must not say: "It is certain that there is a God," but: "I am morally certain that He exists."

In Kant's view, it is essential for my ethical existence and for my faith that I should know *how* I know and *what* I know. I know what is, through what I do. There is "no theoretical faith in the supersensible." Hence: "Unless you first manage to make at least halfway good men of them, you will never make them into sincere believers." It is more in keeping with human nature "to build the expectation of a future world on the feelings of a well-disposed soul than, conversely, to found the good feelings of the soul on the hope of another world."

But knowledge is deceptive: "Knowledge inflates (if it is delusion) but knowledge which reaches to the very limits of knowledge makes for humility." The will to know in realms where only faith can sustain us is itself unbelief. We look for knowledge in the hope of finding a support, of making things easy for ourselves: "Men have a natural leaning to super-stition."

But is it not one of the great evils of our human situation that we can neither prove nor know the existence of God, that God, on the contrary, is so hidden that one who denies Him cannot be compelled by sheer thought to acknowledge Him, while those who believe can only obey the revealed commandments? Would it not be the greatest of gifts to man if God should show Himself, if we could be certain of His existence? Kant replies:

"If God and eternity with their terrible majesty stood perpetually before our eyes (for what we can fully prove has just as much certainty for us as what we can see with our eyes)," then, indeed, men would not transgress the law, His commands would be done. But "most lawful actions would be performed from fear, few from hope, and none at all from duty; the ethical value of actions would thus be transformed into a mere mechanism, just as, in a puppet show, the puppets all gesticulate skillfully but there is no life in the figures. But since He who governs the world permits us only to sur-mise His existence, not to perceive it or clearly prove it, while the ethical law demands our selfless respect, a truly ethical attitude is possible. Thus it may well be true that the unfathomable wisdom through which we exist is no less worthy of our admiration for what it denies us than for what it grants us."

Rational faith is its own source. "Every faith, even historical faith, must indeed be rational (for the ultimate touchstone of truth is always reason), but a rational faith is one which is based on no other data than those con-tained in pure reason."

For Kant, "the principle of the self-preservation of reason" is a bulwark against all perils. It is the foundation of the rational faith in which "cer-tainty is of exactly the same degree as in knowledge, but of a different kind." It draws its strength from the completeness of reason and its tendency to complete itself. Over against it stands the "principle of the self-abandonment of reason." Without pure rational faith, "the use of reason becomes either the pretension to universal knowledge (pansophy) or misology, the suicide of reason."

2. *The Interpretation of Religious Dogmas*
"Within the Limits of Mere Reason"

Man's age-old metaphysical striving is inextinguishable and justified. Even where it errs in its thinking, it is true. "This science, reaching beyond nature, based on pure concepts a priori and therefore called metaphysics, is at the same time the India which promises man far greater and more sumptuous possessions than the wretched homeland of the senses in which he is tyrannized by nature and in the end, after being continuously deluded by the prospect of achieving a final purpose, sees before him nothing but death."

In religion lie the great visions, symbols, and dogmas in which men have found satisfaction. Kant seeks to understand Christian dogma according to his philosophical principles. The speculative dogmas, "it is true, utterly exceed the faculty of human reason," because we can know nothing of objects in the supersensible. But "these rational ideas" have meaning if they are "restricted to the conditions of practical use." That is to say, they are without meaning from the standpoint of knowledge, but they have existential significance. Kant interprets such ideas, mythical conceptions, religious dogmas. He speaks of grace, of the kingdom of God, of the end of all things. He examines the fundamental dogmas of Biblical thinking.

Kant "plays," as he says, "with Ideas that reason creates for itself, whose objects (if they have any) are wholly beyond our scope." They become questionable only when "reason ceases to understand itself and what it wants." For then it "prefers to indulge in futile dreams rather than to remain, as befits an intellectual inhabitant of a sensible world, within the limits of this world."

In interpreting the Biblical conceptions, figures, dogmas "within the limits of mere reason," Kant assumes that there is, at the confines of reason, a realm of the unfathomable and mysterious. But the unfathomable is not the irrational; rather, it is something which reason experiences as the limit of reason and draws into the light of reason. The one, self-elucidating reason does not solve the problems, but acknowledges the mystery. Reason even permits itself to materialize these problems, to state them in terms of thought, and ventures to carry thought, in "analogies," beyond the realm of the knowable; it moves in the play of images. But the images take on truth only through their function in the ethical fulfillment of man. Image and Idea are tested and accepted or rejected, not according to logical cognition but according to ethical reason. For Kant, it is possible to live with these images only within the form of reason. The understanding with its logical reflection acts as judge over dogmatic and mythical figures, but reason as a whole is the area in which they operate and are ethically tested by the essence of the rational men who live by them. Faith is hope when reason shatters against the unfathomable, but it is a hope grounded in reason itself and not in some other guarantee coming from outside. Reason grasps, not being in itself, but being as it becomes accessible to a finite creature in his reason. Hence in Kant—despite formal recognition of the possibility of revelation (the truth of which however is perceived through reason alone)—religion is not an independent source. His work on religion is not a part within the systematic whole of the critical philosophy. But in a way he lived in the aura of the religion that sustained his childhood. He is one of the philosophers in the tradition of Lessing, who rationally interpret the content of religion, who "demythicize" when myth sets itself up as knowledge, but who grasp myth in its essence and so enable us to make it our own.

3. The Universe

Kant does not seek a principle of being, from which everything that is would be derived. Rather, he elucidates the origins of reason and through them makes it clear where we are and how, and what we should do.

The natural conception is very different and quite un-Kantian. Here the universe is a single vast whole, God and world, or only the world. In this view, we see ourselves as a result, not as a source; our knowledge of the world takes the form of cosmologies. Cosmologies are subject to historic change; one differs radically from another. Yet each cosmology is taken as self-evident, not as a cosmology but as being. By knowing all things—the stars, the earth, lifeless matter and life and man—and by knowing man in his history and works, we have being itself, the universe of reality, the world.

Kant endeavors to replace this mode of knowledge by another, which is at once more comprehensive and more moderate in its claims. Kant examines the universe as it appears from the standpoint of our own existence; in fundamental dichotomies, in discovery through actual experience, in the quest of the One. I shall sum up what has been said thus far:

1. The whole world as the universe of cognition is appearance. The "thing in itself" is not a thing but a symbol at the limit of cognition, signifying the phenomenality of all known being. This noumenon (so called in opposition to the phenomenon) is present in our freedom, in the Ideas, in the contemplation of the beautiful. But appearance is not illusion. Science demonstrates its validity ad infinitum. And it points to a ground.

Phenomenon and noumenon represent a fundamental dichotomy; this dichotomy is a theme of philosophy, but in our thinking we cannot adequately objectify it. Appearance itself, in turn, is manifested in dichotomies: sensibility and understanding, being and the ought, nature and freedom.

2. Whatever has being for us must be present to my mind. In my consciousness of my existence I am, as it were, the nodal point in which all dualisms, and particularly nature and freedom, these two modes of being, diverse in origin, are linked. Kant states this in the *Critique of Practical Reason*: "Two things fill the mind with ever new and increasing admiration and awe: the starry heavens above me and the moral law within me." Why these two? "I do not merely conjecture and seek them as though obscured in darkness or in the transcendent region beyond my horizon: I see them before me, and I *associate them directly with the consciousness of my own existence.*" How so? "The former begins at the place I occupy in the external world of sense, and it broadens the connection in which I stand into an unbounded magnitude of worlds beyond worlds and systems of systems and

into the limitless times of their periodic motion, their beginning and their continuance. The latter begins at my invisible self, my personality, and exhibits me in a world which has true infinity but which is comprehensible only to the understanding—a world with which I recognize myself as existing in a universal and necessary (and not only, as in the first case, contingent) connection." What is the consequence of this for my consciousness of being? "The former view of a countless multitude of worlds annihilates, as it were, my importance as an animal creature, which must give back to the planet (a mere speck in the universe) the matter from which it came, the matter which is for a little time provided with vital force, we know not how. The latter, on the contrary, infinitely raises my worth as that of an intelligence by my personality, in which the moral law reveals a life independent of all animality and even of the whole sensuous world."

3. Since my being in the world is not one, but split, since the universe is divided into nature and freedom, I seek the One. Is there a One? In the area where we stand and are, the One speaks through the dichotomies, but also through our intimations of ways in which they may be transcended.

Through all Kant's philosophizing runs a search for the "middle term" between the categories and sensibility, the imagination; between the universal and the particular, the reflecting judgment; between reason and the understanding, the schema of the Idea; between nature and freedom, the contemplation of the beautiful. This middle term is always found by operations of the understanding—yet it is never a known object, but a mode in which something which "in itself" remains hidden is manifested to us.

Wherever Kant fixates dualities, he raises the question of the link between them, the middle term. The middle term is present in the actuality of the individual and as the supersensible One, which is disclosed in it. To the dogmatic who considers the dualities as indispensable positions and sources of clarity, the middle term seems to be a leap into the bottomless abyss or a disclosure of the hidden root from which everything springs. But the middle term does not negate the dualities. In penetrating the dualities, it aims to elucidate the riddle, not to solve it. Once fully known, the middle term would be meaningless.

Does Kantian thinking permit us to conceive of a supersensible One which splits in two and then, in its ultimate dichotomy, the knowledge and action of man, finds the turnabout that will carry it back to itself? No, a metaphysical idea of this kind would be objective, not critical; it would be in keeping with Plotinus, not with Kant. In such a conception the totality of being is a process, and man occurs at a determinate point in it. For Kant such ideas are play. His perspective remains that of man; he does not set himself up in an illusory realm outside of man, whence man, like a God, might survey the whole or recapitulate God's thoughts. Kant never succumbs to the illusion of overstepping the possibilities of man. He does not desert from the ranks of mankind.

V. KANTIAN REASON

Reason is not comparable to individual character, which varies with each person; it is the character of man as such, which can only be one. It is the intelligible character. In the phenomenal world, this intelligible character is a mentality, which produces itself from itself, and it is the will which holds fast to its own reason in the form of invariable principles prescribed by it. The mentality is not given by nature; it must be elaborated in time, through freedom.

1. *The Revolution in Thinking*

Philosophy was for Kant a "revolution in man's way of thinking." From time immemorial it had been a "way," which was to be found by a turnabout. This, in a new form and perhaps more radically than ever before, was true also for Kant. For him the "way" became a movement leading to revolution and a never-ending task after the revolution. And it was through his philosophy of the way that Kant arrived at the way which he traveled in his life.

A. *Kant's way:* We have described Kant's way to critical philosophy. The substance, grounded in the Biblical tradition, had always been the same. But in the course of his philosophizing Kant arrived at a new understanding of it, recast it and made it into the essence of philosophizing itself. Despite all the documents relating to it, Kant's development as a whole remains a mystery. But we must examine it and gain some understanding of it if we are not to lose sight of the foundation, the aim, and the scope of his thinking, if we are not to mistake supposed Kantian positions for the essence of his philosophy.

Certain points stand out as essential. In the 1770 dissertation, he anticipated the "Transcendental Aesthetic" of the *Critique of Pure Reason* (1781; the doctrine of the subjectivity and a priori character of space and time as the forms of intuition). But in the dissertation there is no mention yet of the subjectivity of the categories as the function constitutive of the objectivity of the whole world of experience. However, though this great idea may be said to sustain the whole of Kant's critical philosophy, it cannot be singled out as the new element in Kantian thinking.

Consequently, a whole decade was needed before Kant came into the full movement of his thought, where everything was recast in a new vision, which is vastly more than any definite idea. To be sure, the demonstrable steps taken in the pre-critical works are in themselves "critical" operations, always relating to particular formulations of problems, but they are not elements in the total critique from which the later philosophy grew. What he acquired in the pre-critical period was in large part retained, but it was not yet the philosophy. The new element cannot be derived from all these separate ideas. The transcendental method, which Kant calls "critical," is not the result of a number of discoveries. It is a leap. Whither it would lead was still unclear, perhaps necessarily so, but it was the source of astounding clarities. The leap cannot be localized in time.

Indeed we seem, in the pre-critical works, to sense none of the amazing power of the Kantian philosophy. They lack the sheer conceptual vigor of the later works; they do not, like the later works, illumine immeasurable depths with clear concepts. For the style of the great critical works is marked by the weight and depth of their content.

The new mode of thought did not come to Kant through a revelation, nor through a decisive insight, nor through his creative genius, nor in a particular month or year; it resulted from a fundamental attitude (described by Kant himself), which made it possible for his insights to develop. It was a systematic procedure; once it was there, the necessary steps came of themselves. At first it dealt in particulars, but then it found itself in a totality where, to Kant's amazement, the particulars hung together. He had marked off a field containing vast possibilities pointing to further possibilities at its limits.

Now Kant had certainty. He knew he had discovered an infinitely productive method of philosophizing. This is what would make him a seminal thinker in the eyes of all who have understood him. Even before his thinking was at an end, he was able to say: Just as we are in a position to begin properly we must step aside.

Kant's "way" is first his way to this philosophy, but also it is the philosophy itself as a way, which by the very nature of things could not attain its end. It seems possible that an understanding of the philosophy requires an understanding of the way in which he came to it.

B. *Revolution in ethical thinking:* The revolution in thinking is the essence of reason itself. What happens in philosophical thought has its model and its echo in the ethical. Man does not derive the character of which as a rational being he becomes aware "from nature"; "he must at all times acquire it."

The founding of a character may "resemble a kind of rebirth. A solemn resolution makes the time when the transformation took place in him unforgettable, a new epoch." The origin is the decision, but the decision is embedded in the whole of his life. "Any fragmentary attempt to become a better man is futile." The foundation of a character lies in the "absolute unity of the inner principle of a man's whole life conduct." "No doubt," says Kant, "there are few men who have attempted this revolution before the thirtieth year, and still fewer who have firmly established it before their fortieth."

c. *The aim:* Such a transformation of outlook is immensely difficult. After a clear objective insight, the individual, in every case, demands the impossible: to transcend the objective by means of a dialectic.

This would be mere eccentricity if it were an arbitrary feature of Kantian thinking. His opponents accuse him of fostering subjectivization, phenomenologization, a negation of objectivity, or of claiming to carry out operations that are impossible. What is new in Kant, they say, is a total error. But in reply it can be said: The new insight, derived from the nature of our reason, is merely a new way of raising to consciousness something that men have known for thousands of years.

Those who accept the new insight regard it as the condition of all human truth. But they must not close their eyes to the fact that there are others who do not understand it. Kant's fundamental new insight clarifies the situation of man: it shows us that we can discern the limits of every mode of thought. But the way does not lead to a land where everything is well ordered, known, enumerable. The order of the Kantian system is only an order in which there is room for all "ways," not a fulfillment and completion. Kant leads us to a realm where life perpetually brings forth new life, into the secret of the creative sources of reason. Those who follow him must go there in person and do what Kant did not do for them. Kant gives them the opportunity.

The "new science" is extraordinary and demands the extraordinary. "My book," writes Kant (May 11, 1781), "can produce nothing other than a total change in outlook in this area of human knowledge." "What I am working on in the *Critique* is not metaphysics, but a totally new and hitherto unattempted science, namely the critique of a reason that judges a priori." Kant calls his new thinking a "metaphysics of metaphysics." By way of analogy to the revolution brought about by the great astronomer, Kant called his innovation in the realm of knowledge a "Copernican revolution": no longer, as in all previous conceptions, do concepts take their form from objects; now, on the contrary, objects take their form from concepts.

But there is more to the revolution than that. The new thinking is all-encompassing. For it illuminates the whole of reason. Everything that can enter man's mind is affected; everything demands a new form and a new atmosphere in the manner of its being thought. Accordingly, even the first preparatory sketches speak not only of knowledge but also of ethics and taste and the ultimate purposes of mankind. Then, in the seventies, he concentrated on the foundation, which is formulated in the *Critique of Pure Reason*. But it was soon followed by the other critical works which do justice to the original broader conception.

2. The Scope of Kant's Questioning

Philosophizing is a striving to clarify a whole which in the beginning is obscure. Hence it must differentiate, think the parts successively, and in this movement build up the whole.

From the moment it begins to build, my thinking must contain within it what it is looking for. This means that I must enter into it with my whole being: I must make a leap. Suddenly I see before me what in my thinking will begin to grow by taking on clarity. Thus the essential in this play of question and answer is not the object but the direction. The first clarity begins with the question. The question determines the meaning of philosophizing. Kant's celebrated fundamental questions, which he repeats over and over and which determine his whole philosophy, may be developed as follows:

1. Our natural attitude is this: In my thinking, being confronts me as an object. I take it as it is given to me. Being is being-known. It is "in itself" as it is for me. I take this for granted, but not consciously so; that is, I do not inquire into my tacit assumption. But then—and this is an important step—the natural attitude becomes unsure of itself. This is what has been happening in modern philosophy since Descartes. A question is raised. Kant carries it to the very heart of the matter: how does the thinking subject come to the thought object? How are the two related? Surely I, the thinker, am not the object that I think. What then is the relation between thinking and what is thought? Kant's first fundamental question is: *What can I know?*

2. I act because I want something. Why do I want something? In order to live or because it gives me pleasure or because it interests me. But what then? I ask whether life, pleasure, interest are worth while, I ask after the meaning and the purpose and the final purpose that will first give meaning to the whole. In other words, I ask whether, as though deluded by purposes without a final purpose, my will is contingent, directed at random toward this or that, or whether I can will unconditionally because there is no deeper ground that needs inquiring into; or whether my will can be not provisional but definitive, not contingent but necessary, not because someone else says so, but because an unconditionally binding commandment is addressed directly to me. Kant's second question: *What should I do?*

3. The consequences of action in accordance with the unconditional law do not by any means coincide with the happiness that I desire. The world is full of injustice, absurdity, contingency. Since my understanding is certain only of what I know within the limits of possible experience, and since it is from a different source that my practical reason determines what I should do, I am left with a profound dissatisfaction. The whole of being is grasped neither by my knowledge nor my will. Being is split for me. Unity, the harmony between the parts that are separate in temporal existence, can reside only in the supersensible. Kant's third question: *What may I hope for?*

4. To these questions Kant, in two passages, added a fourth: *What is man?* He says: Fundamentally, one might subsume the first three questions under the last. The fourth question, which in Kant's words encompasses the other three, means that Kant does not start from God, being, the world, the

object, or the subject, but from man, for man is the area in which all the rest become reality for us. It is in our own existence, through our experience or action, that we must test what is true. But the priority of the fourth question does not mean that the knowledge of being is to be replaced by the knowledge of man. Being remains the essential, but man can approach and apprehend it only through his existence as a man. The question does not imply that Kant has a definitive answer. Man is not subsumed under something else; in essence he is not a species in a genus including other species known to us. He is the medium of reality in which what is possible for us is situated.

From the very beginning, this question was the driving force in Kant's philosophizing. In the pre-critical period, he wrote: "If there is any science man really needs it is the one I am teaching, namely, the science which shows man how to occupy worthily the place allotted to him in Creation, the science from which he can learn what a man must be in order to be a man." But this question was not, like the first three, answered in a special work. Kant's *Anthropology,* a collection, published in his old age, of lectures he had delivered over a period of many years, does not provide an answer adequate to his understanding of the question. This book, treating anthropology "in a pragmatic sense," is of great interest, but disappointing in view of the magnitude of the question. Kant's real answer to this fourth fundamental question was the whole of his work.

These four questions taken together mark off "the field of philosophy in its cosmopolitan significance." In the actual construction of his system Kant formulated his questions much more precisely, as for example: How are synthetic judgments a priori possible? But the great fundamental questions have the priority; it is they that determine the content of the philosophizing and of the precise, strictly formulated questions. For the discipline of philosophy can have meaning only if it serves to form men of "cosmopolitan" scope, citizens of the world.

What is the meaning of philosophical questioning? We tend to expect answers such as are given in the sciences: answers which inform me about something; or technical prescriptions that show me how to make something. But philosophical questions and answers give us something very different.

In philosophical questions I transcend every object, all determinate existence, every definite representation of the world, I refuse to anticipate the validity of any prescribed architecture of the world, of any determinate action or aims. But in thus transcending all particular objectivities, I must not set them aside as indifferent, as though true being were somewhere else. For if I wish to think, being is accessible to me only in objectivity. In my transcending I should, rather, look for what we call the source or origin, from which, although it is never an object, all objects, all frameworks of objectivity, all horizons into which I enter, first derive the possibility of their particular existence.

Thus the ultimate aim of philosophizing is a question and, what is more, a question to which no answer is possible. In opposition to this thesis, it has been argued that such questioning is futile, that a question which cannot be answered should not be asked. This argument applies the requirements of scientific knowledge to philosophizing. For it is implicit in the transcending (and hence philosophical) character of such questions that they cannot, like scientific questions, be defined in terms of exact concepts.

Philosophical questions have a different kind of clarity. What matters is how the question is developed, what happens when it is answered or not answered, how the question becomes the source of a movement of thought, which reason translates into an inner action identical with the thought itself. With all this, we gain no knowledge of an object, but our consciousness of being is transformed. A philosophical question becomes as meaningless as its object if it is denatured into scientific objectivity. Its meaning lies in its direction, even if no clear answer is given, or perhaps just because no answer is given. For there is a radical difference between the mere knowledge of the understanding and an illumination through reason of our understanding at its limit. The nonknowledge of the understanding remains purely negative, it leaves the mind empty. The nonknowledge of philosophical exploration transcends the understanding and transforms our awareness of being; it leaves us richer in our thinking and open to new thinking.

3. *Kant's Skepticism*

Kant's cast of mind was never truly skeptical. From the beginning he was at peace with the traditional ideas. But they did not suffice him. He wished to know. He refused to accept a belief because it was accepted by men of good character or because famous men had professed it. He inquired into the grounds of the knowledge expressed in faith. From the standpoint of knowledge, many propositions that were taken as self-evident, and particularly those dealing with essential contents such as God and immortality, struck him as questionable. But the foundations of his being were not shaken by his questioning. He seemed to be developing into a serene skeptic. But this was not his aim. He had no desire whatever to fall into the skepticism in which reason has always been tempted to find an easy bed. What he wanted was to attain, through skepticism, to true certainty. But the certainty he was after did not relate to method or to particular questions in the world, or to any revelation. He sought certainty in a knowledge relating to the whole of our rational existence, to the possibilities and limits of reason in its multidimensional yet coherent totality.

Kant attained certainty in thinking on the basis of a conviction that had sustained him from the start. With his *Critique of Pure Reason* he acquired a foundation that he regarded as absolutely solid. He was certain of having marked off the limits of reason, according to secure principles, in such a way "that in future men will be able to know with certainty whether the ground they stand on is one of reason or of sophistry." As early as 1773, he wrote confidently that he hoped "to give philosophy an enduring new turn that would be far more advantageous to religion and morals."

Through Kant's whole work runs the justification of objectivity as universal validity. This objectivity is found in subjectivity, but no less is subjectivity determined by objectivity. Thus in Kant everything is subjective, because, in the phenomenal world of our existence, it is conditioned by the subjectivity of our reason, but also objective, because it springs from the source.

Lest we be misled by the word "subjectivity," we must first exclude all private subjectivity as the manifold of the individual. Kant's subjectivity is common, hence communicative and public. It is the subject of the cognitive "consciousness as such," and it extends to the subjectivity of empirical sociability and its rules, which have their meaning in the communicability of feelings.

All certainty is in judgments. Judgment is the act in which we gain a valid awareness of being by joining two separate representations in a unity. But what Kant calls judgment is not only an act of thought expressed in a proposition. There is also the empirical judgment in which, through perception, we gain valid knowledge of an object; there is the practical judgment, which becomes clear as an ethical imperative; there is the judgment of taste in the contemplation of the beautiful, which is never expressed in a proposition of thought, but has its predicate in a valid feeling of pleasure or pain (a universally valid feeling rather than a universally valid concept). In all three directions, subjective judgments (without universal validity) must be distinguished from objectively valid judgments: aesthetic sensible judgments of the pleasant from aesthetic reflecting judgments; mere judgments of perception from empirical judgments; technical and pragmatic imperatives from the categorical imperative.

4. *Negative and Positive Significance of Philosophizing*

There is a twofold motivation in Kant, toward cognition as advancing scientific knowledge in the world, and toward freedom as the presence of true being, of which we achieve certainty in its enactment. He insists that the two should not be confused, that I should not desire to know what I cannot know, that I should not delude myself with pseudo knowledge and so destroy my freedom.

This is why critical safeguards play so great a part in Kant's thinking. Kant was able to say: "The whole philosophy of true reason is directed solely toward this negative benefit." Where illusion is made inevitable by the nature of reason, critical elucidation can prevent us from letting ourselves be deceived by the illusion, even though the illusion cannot be dispelled, just as sensory illusions may persist even after we have recognized them, but deceive us no longer.

Philosophy as transcendental insight is no longer ontology (which "proud name" Kant explicitly rejects for his thinking), but critique. It differentiates and defines the limits of our faculties, through which our consciousness and action are constituted in the modes in which being can be present for us.

The world is our one and only field of knowledge, but knowledge of the world is not knowledge of being. Knowledge of being (ontology) is impossible; it is replaced by transcendental philosophy: Kant does not rise to another world, but presses to the limit of all existence. This transcending does not take him to another realm, but a transcending it remains, because it is a totally different operation from any that we perform in our knowledge of the world.

Misinterpretation of this Kantian thinking can result in two perversions: we slip back into the world, as though Kant were concerned only with a theory of knowledge by which to justify the validity of science—or we slip back into the old metaphysics (e.g., the theory that the world is dream and illusion). In the first case we lose transcendence, in the second we lose the world. But in Kant the two are inseparable; the world is not illusion but appearance; the phenomenal world is not intrinsic being, but it is the language of transcendence.

Yet we chafe at our limitations. We should like to have the truth in a more concrete, effective, perfect form than the form that is granted us. We intoxicate ourselves with an ecstatic absolute, neglect the knowledge that is possible for us, and submerge our own selves in the intensity of our illusion.

Materialization of the supersensible quells the power of freedom. That, says Kant, is why governments, in order to have passive subjects, have encouraged religion to fit itself out with all sort of "childish trappings" and "accessories." In this way they spare the subject the trouble, but also deprive him of the possibility, of extending his intellectual powers beyond the limits arbitrarily imposed on him, that make him easy to handle.

Kant's only irreconcilable adversaries are those who, on the ground that reason has limits, strive not only to remain within them but to destroy reason altogether through an irrational objectivization which necessarily goes hand in hand with spiritual violence. Reason sacrifices, abjures itself. Kant deals with this immemorial antagonism to reason under the titles: maundering (*Schwärmerei*), fanaticism, dogmatism.

By "maundering" Kant meant: to transgress the limits of human reason in pursuit of principles. "To see something beyond the limits of the sensible world, i.e., to dream according to principles [with a kind of raving reason]" is a delusion. It is moral maundering to base ethical action on the supposed possession of holiness and purity of heart. It is "the inflated, high-flown, fanciful mentality" of those who base their action on surgings of the heart rather than on duty, and so forget their duty. Religious maundering is the notion that effects of grace can be distinguished from effects of virtue, that grace can be counted on to engender virtuous action, and, finally, that we can exert an influence on the supersensible object.

Kant's philosophy seems to impoverish us. It seems to demolish everything that was dear to the metaphysical needs of man and even the possibility of happiness in the world. But it derives an incomparable power from the critical discipline with which it guides me to the limits of existence in order that I should live uprightly in my existence. By his elucidaton of reason, Kant enjoins us to be wholly present in the world and in our inner lives, to do what lies within our possibilities, and not to neglect it for the sake of pleasing illusions. And in disclosing the limits of reason, he teaches us to content ourselves with the existence allotted to us, to respect the limits of reason, yet do our utmost to extend them. That is what Kant meant when he said: You cannot "learn philosophy but only how to philosophize." And: "Philosophy consists in knowing our limits."

Our secret yearning for material possession of the essential may lead us to feel that pure reason is powerless. Kant's view of reason, which, through the moral law, the Ideas, life, and the beautiful, brings home to him his bond with God, is the very opposite: it is in reason that he sees the veritable power. "Perhaps there is no more sublime passage in the Law of the Jews than the commandment: Thou shalt not make unto thee any graven image or any likeness. . . . The same applies to the idea of the moral law. There is no ground for the apprehension that if it were stripped of everything that can commend it to the senses, it would carry only a cold and lifeless sanction and lose its dynamic force." It is not true that the nonsensuous is without power. For where the senses perceive nothing, but the inextinguishable idea of morality remains alive, its power is unconquerable.

The world is not the whole. There is a realm of spirits, that is, of rational beings who through reason know of each other. However, it exists only as a realm of freedom to be realized in time, not as an intelligible other world and not as an objective institution in this world, but only as an invisible Church. This realm of spirits, this invisible Church, is the foundation of hope in this world. This great unorganized and unorganizable community is the source of salvation.

5. *The Finiteness of Man and the Limits of Reason*

Kantian reason views itself as the supreme authority which produces itself and thereby man. Is this overweening pride? That is the theological criticism of Kant. In answer it may be said: *First,* Kantian reason must not be confused with the mere understanding or with mere opinion. But *secondly,* and above all: In its bringing forth, Kantian reason is conscious of receiving: as understanding, it receives the experience of the sensible world, and even as reason in the strict sense, it receives the objectivity of the Ideas and at its limits receives the supersensible. Kantian reason is not self-sufficient, although in the world, in our temporal, phenomenal existence, it is the indispensable condition of authentic and reliable certainty. For reason, precisely because it is reason, knows the finiteness of man and is aware of its own limits.

A. *The finiteness of man:* Man is finite, because he is always dependent on something other and because he is in no respect absolutely perfectible. Our understanding is discursive, not intuitive; it produces its object in respect to its form, but not in respect to its existence; it is dependent on experience and can never conclude the process of its knowledge.

Our will is imperfect, because its satisfaction is dependent on the existence of an object. Our physical needs make us finite.

No man can rely on himself alone. Everyone is dependent on others. We are men only through our community with men. There is no possible self-sufficiency of the individual.

Finite but rational beings can never be wholly content with their whole existence, for that would presuppose a consciousness of self-sufficiency. Hence we long to be happy, but can never be so definitively and completely.

Finiteness is temporality. So long as there is temporality, there is no standing still. Our rational existence is not the infinity of a perfect, eternal present but a never completed *progressus*. For us "rational but finite beings, only a *progressus ad infinitum* is possible."

All the characteristics of our finiteness culminate in the fact that for us, as rational, sensuous beings, the dichotomy between nature and freedom cannot be overcome. The necessity of the natural laws has not the slightest connection with the necessity of the moral laws, as far as their consequences are concerned. There is no adequate relation between our happiness as beings belonging partly to the world and the consequences of the actions we perform through our good will in obedience to the law. Consequently, our inclination to happiness is cut off from our duty in pursuing the moral law. In our finite existence, our morality remains a struggle with ourselves and the world. In this cleavage we are capable of the autonomy of reason, but not of the autocracy of an undivided holy essence.

Holiness "would be the complete adequacy of the will to the moral law, a perfection of which no rational being in the material world is capable at any moment in his existence." Our morality is not the holiness of our being, but obedience to duty. We finite beings must represent the ethical laws as commandments: Our reason cannot express the necessity of the ethical law as being (happening), but only as a "should be." In an undivided intelligible world, there would be no difference between duty and action, nor between the value of actions of good will and their fortunate or unfortunate consequences in reality.

The struggle of the finite ethical being is enacted in the good will. It is directed toward "virtue," which is its own purpose and also its own reward. And so radiant is the ideal of virtue, "that in the eyes of man it seems to overshadow even the obscure holiness that is never tempted to transgress." But this is "none the less a delusion," because in it "we mistake the subjective conditions by which we estimate greatness for the objective condition of greatness as such."

Because "in respect to holiness our only possibility is a progress ad infinitum," the attitude that befits us is "self-respect tempered by humility." The Stoic attitude of supposing that perfect virtue is "attainable in this life" represents a failure to recognize our finite nature. Among men we may find examples, but never archetypes of virtue. Only the Idea can give us inner guidance. We have no other standard of our actions than "this divine man within us, with whom we compare ourselves." "But to attempt to embody the Idea in an example, as one might embody the wise man in a novel, is unseemly, and moreover there is something absurd and hardly edifying about it, for our natural limitations which persistently interfere with the perfection of the Idea, forbid all illusion about such an attempt and thereby cast suspicion even on the good that lies in the Idea and make it seem like a mere imagining."

Man's character as a rational, finite being also provides an answer to the question of whether he is good or evil by nature. Through his *intelligible* character, man is good. Experience, however, discloses an inclination to evil as soon as man begins to make use of his freedom. Thus man "in regard to his *sensible* character is to be judged as evil, but there is no contradiction between these statements."

B. *The limits of reason:* Reason can elucidate itself but cannot know whence it comes. Nor can it derive itself from a first principle, whether given or resulting from logical operations or from experience.

1. *The fundamental faculties cannot be derived:* "All human insight is at an end once we come to the fundamental powers or faculties; for their possibility can be understood through nothing else, but no more may it be invented or postulated arbitrarily." We know the fundamental theoretical faculties of reason in that they are confirmed by experience, but our understanding is powerless to explain the fact that there are two forms of intuition (space and time) and that there are certain definite categories and forms of judgment and just these. As for the faculties of practical reason, the moral law can only be taken "as a kind of fact"; it is known a priori and apodictically certain, although it cannot be demonstrated by any experience.

2. *The incomprehensibility of freedom:* Though postulated on the basis of the moral law, freedom is beyond our comprehension. We cannot theoretically understand how freedom is possible; that is, we can form no positive representation of this mode of causality. It is something that no human understanding will ever fathom, and yet, even in the basest of men it is a conviction that no sophistry will ever dispel.

It is impossible to explain how a will can be governed directly by a law, how the moral law can act upon feeling, set a limit to self-love and self-complacency, and engender a sense of respect and humility. Time and again, Kant expresses his amazement: How is it possible "that the mere idea of a universal law should be a more powerful determinant for the will than any conceivable motives derived from advantage?" Reason cannot grasp it, and no examples from experience can prove that it must be so. The law commands unconditionally. "Even if there had never been a man who obeyed this law unconditionally," "the objective necessity of being such a man would be undiminished and self-evident."

After formulating the categorical imperative, Kant tells us that the possibility or necessity of an a priori proposition of this kind had never been proved. He himself never claimed to prove it. The most that could be clearly understood was the analytical proposition: If morality is not a chimerical idea without truth, it necessarily implies the autonomy of the will. What, then, is the source of our certainty of the moral law? It can only be practical, grounded in action.

Once we have defined the limit of ethical insight, we are safe from two errors: *First error:* Our reason searches the sensible world for an ultimate cause of ethical action and a comprehensible empirical interest, thus losing its self-understanding. *Second error:* Our reason limits itself to the "intelligible world," where it flutters about helplessly amid transcendent concepts and phantasms, powerless to make the slightest advance.

3. *Conversion from evil:* The extreme limit of reason is the impossibility of understanding radical evil and conversion from evil. What Kant calls radical evil is embodied in the maxim that comes to a rational and sensuous being with the first awareness of his freedom: I will comply with the moral law only on condition that it promote my happiness. It is a reversal of the true maxim: I will strive for happiness only on condition that my action does not offend against the moral law.

The rational origin of radical evil is unfathomable for us, because we are held responsible for being evil, and yet evil is originally inherent in human nature. "The possibility that a naturally evil man should make himself into a good man surpasses all our understanding." But since we "ought" to turn away from evil, we must be able to.

It is in the area of this incomprehensibility that we must situate the myth of original sin and the notion of grace. Reason does not deny the possibility of the objects of these religious conceptions. However, it cannot include them in its maxims of thought and action, but must find the ground of its actions within itself. Any recourse to something outside it would weaken it. Nothing must alleviate its extreme exertion. But it knows its limit and recognizes that some things are beyond comprehension.

Accordingly, reason does not contest the supersensible possibility of help through grace, but conceives of grace as a supplement to its own insufficiency. Reason even hopes "that if in the unfathomable realm of the supernatural there is something more than reason can explain, it may, even though unknown, come to the help of the rational good will"—though this additional support is not regarded as a possession. A rational faith of this kind may be called a "reflecting faith" (a faith that reflects on possibilities), "because the dogmatic faith which sets itself up as a knowledge strikes it as dishonest or presumptuous."

For us, reason must rely on itself. Does this mean that it owes everything to itself? Yes, as far as its exertions are concerned—no, in regard to its own unfathomable limit. After doing all it can, it hopes for outside help, but grace must not be a condition of its activity nor an object of its concern, for grace is something that reason can neither know nor control. "To anticipate an effect of grace would mean that the good is not our act but the act of another being, and consequently that we can come by it only by doing nothing, which is a contradiction."

4. *For and against reason:* Is there a higher authority above reason, a deeper source of truth? If so, is it myth, is it revelation? Here men are divided. Some demand an attitude of faith and acceptance toward the historically determined manifestation of a super-reason which thought can elucidate but not test. Others recognize no higher authority than reason taken in the broadest sense. Though reason is wholly receptive, they hold, it is receptive by virtue of its spontaneity. It remains the indispensable medium of verification and in this temporal existence there can be no better one. It bars the way to blind obedience, that is to say, to an obedience without thought or an obedience that restricts thought.

All independent philosophy since antiquity has pressed the lofty claim of reason, but with Kant the concept of reason acquired an unprecedented depth. In the movement of his thinking as a whole, he seems to know more than he can reveal. That is why, though in all his thinking Kant strove for lucidity, transparency, precision, clearsighted men have been filled with awe and wonder by his philosophy, as by a mystery, yet others have repudiated Kant for his contradictions and because he made them feel forsaken; for it seemed to them that he always took away what he had just given.

VI. POLITICS AND HISTORY

Kant did not deal with politics in compendious works comparable to those devoted to the origins and limits of reason. But the numerous short treatises and the remarks in the larger works demonstrate, by their continuity, that Kant had far more than an incidental interest in politics. A philosophy whose first and last question treats of man is bound to be deeply concerned with politics. And indeed, Kant was a political thinker of the first rank.

Kant's philosophy is intended for all men; it aspires to teach them how to occupy the place allotted to man in the universe. His politics conceives the well-being of men in the world; rejecting all utopias and ideologies, it seeks to determine what is possible and what is right in the human situation.

In his political thinking, Kant develops the idea of a realization of reason. "Man is destined by his reason to live in a society with men and in it to cultivate, civilize, and moralize himself by means of art and the sciences." In other words, man does not start out as what he *is,* but must make himself into what he *ought to be.* His animal inclination "to give himself passively to the charms of comfort" may be great. His rational task is "actively, in battle against obstacles, to make himself worthy of mankind."

The realization of reason is determined by two complementary considerations: on the one hand, the order of all, on the other, the fulfillment of each individual. On the one hand, man's mission is a "cosmopolitan society" (or: "The kingdom of God on earth: that is the ultimate mission"). On the other hand, the dignity of man requires a form of community in which he as a man is not subject to other men, but asserts his freedom as an individual. "A dependent man ceases to be a man." "No misfortune is more terrible than to find myself at the mercy of a creature of my own kind, who can compel me to surrender to his caprice and do his will."

1. *The Fundamental Ideas*

A. History presents a bleak picture. It discloses no rule. The actions of men seem to reveal neither instinct nor plan. "We cannot dispel a certain indignation when we observe what they have done and left undone on the great stage of the world; and though here and there we find apparent wisdom in the particular, the whole seems to be a tissue of folly, childish vanity, and often of childish malice and love of destruction."

B. In human society as such Kant finds insoluble antinomies:

1. Nature and culture are in constant conflict. Man dies or becomes feeble with age just as he seems to have prepared himself for the greatest discoveries. His lifetime does not suffice for the fulfillment of what he has undertaken. His accomplishment is fragmentary and there is no assurance that it will endure after him. The inequality among men cannot be dispelled by culture. It is a source of good and of much evil.

2. Man is a creature who needs a master. But those who play the part of masters, because they are men, also need masters. Where is the master to whom a ruler must feel subordinate if he is to be capable of ruling properly? "Man must be educated toward the good; but the educator himself can only be a man."

3. An individual can preserve a community by acting well only if the other acts well. The result is a circle of reciprocity. "The first spur to evil

is that even if one wishes to be good one cannot be sure that others harbor the same wish. No one wishes to be good all by himself. A scoundrel, if he lived entirely among kindly, honorable people, would cast off his malice." The good in the individual can be created only by the universal, but the good cannot become universal without the individual.

4. Man as an individual claims to be a purpose in himself and a fulfillment. But the destiny of man is fulfilled only in the course of history by the race as a whole. Epochs and individuals are stages in a process which is perhaps a progress.

c. *The fundamental question:* Kant finds evil in the general aspect of history and in the insoluble antinomies of human society. But this is not his last word. Quite on the contrary, it is the starting point of his political thinking. The vision of evil remains undispelled, but it perpetually engenders the fundamental question regarding the meaning of history and political action.

Accordingly, Kant inquires into the purpose and meaning of historical events. We see purposiveness in the organisms. In the wonderful diversity of its forms, living nature displays so much purposiveness that the religious mind attributes it to God's creative will. But "what does it avail us to praise the glory and wisdom of Creation in the reasonless realm of nature, if the history of the human race never ceases to belie" the purpose of Creation, if "the sight of this vast theater of divine wisdom compels us to avert our eyes in indignation, to despair of finding fulfillment of a rational purpose in this world and to defer all hope of it to the next?"

Kant replies with another question: Is it "rational to suppose that nature is purposive in its parts but without purpose in the whole?" The organisms (things which are also natural purposes) show that there is a purposiveness in parts of the universe. And so Kant goes on to ask whether a "natural purpose," an ultimate meaning, may not be concealed in the blind contingency of history, though when we survey the general course of history, no such meaning is discernible. From this question springs Kant's philosophy of history and politics.

The general attitude behind the philosophy is easy to understand, but hard to formulate in clear concepts. The ideas reflect all the tensions inherent in the theme. A number of statements contradict each other if singled out and taken by themselves. In the general context, the contradictions are resolved, but there is nowhere a finished synthesis or global view. Nevertheless, let us try to discern the simplicity of the outlook in the dialectic complexity of Kant's political thinking. We shall follow out the central themes one by one.

D. *Nature and freedom:* Amid the general absurdity of human affairs, Kant looks for a natural purpose "which would make a history according to a determinate plan of nature possible for creatures who act without any plan of their own." He looks for the natural purpose behind the genesis and progress of the human race.

We know nothing about the "hypothetical beginning of human history." Taking Genesis, Chapters 2-4, as his guide, Kant constructs (quite aware that he is undertaking "a mere pleasure trip").

He starts with a fully fashioned man, who can stand, walk, and talk. What happens then? Human thought explores the given world, extends the horizon, engenders infinite possibilities:

1. Man's whole life, like that of the animals, is governed by the instincts. But his thinking reaches out ahead of them. His knowledge of foodstuffs, by way of analogy, amplifies his nutritive instinct. By trial and error he develops the faculty of choosing his mode of life, and is no longer, like the animals, confined to a single mode of life. Thought transforms the sexual instinct, which in the animal is a passing periodic urge, removes its object from the senses, so prolonging and enhancing the stimulus to the imagination, and moderates it, so preventing the satiety and disgust which are the end of the animal's desire. A great step forward was the refusal which transformed desire into love. 2. Thinking, man comes to regard himself as the purpose of nature, and to look on everything else, everything that is not a rational being, as a means. "The first time he said to a sheep: Nature gave you your fleece not for yourself but for me, and removed it and put it on his own back, he became aware of a privilege that raised him over all the animals." But at the same time, the thought emerged that it was not permissible to say any such thing to a man. The claim to be a purpose in himself is the foundation of the unlimited equality of men. 3. Thinking, man acquires the possibility of anticipating the future and the knowledge of death—great steps forward, which are at the same time an inexhaustible source of care, anxiety, and fear.

With all these steps, man has been expelled from his animal state, the paradise which provided for his needs with no effort on his part. He is thrust out into the wide world. Often the hardship of his life tempts him to wish that he were back in paradise, dreaming his life away in tranquil idleness and eternal peace. "But between him and the imagined abode of bliss stands his restless reason, irresistibly driving him to develop the capacities with which he is endowed, and forbidding any return to the state of savagery and simplicity." The step from paradise is a step from guidance by animal instinct to guidance by reason, from the tutelage of nature to a state of freedom. At first the progress of the species is not an improvement for the individual, who is beset by vices that were unknown to him in his state of ignorance. Man's first step is an ethical fall, while physically it is marked by all manner of evils. "The history of nature thus begins with the good, for it is the work of God; the history of freedom begins with evil, for it is the work of man."

There is—here Kant agreed with Rousseau—an inevitable conflict between culture and nature. But it is only through this conflict that man can develop all his powers and faculties and progress toward rational freedom. Kant therefore held that Rousseau was wrong in demanding a return to nature. Calamity, vice, evil spur man to improve himself.

The continuation of the process thus begun is history. Kant looks for a "natural purpose" in the history of man. First he shows that a being endowed with the faculty of reason must have a history. The teleological doctrine of nature presupposes that all a creature's natural dispositions are destined, at some time, to develop in accordance with a purpose. The specific natural dispositions of man are attuned to the use of his reason. Whereas the natural dispositions of animals develop fully in the individual, that of man, reason, can only achieve full development in the course of the generations, in the species. For reason—the faculty of extending the rules and purposes governing the use of all his powers "far beyond the scope of natural instinct"—requires experiment, practice, and instruction. Nature never makes a superfluous move. In giving man reason instead of instinct, nature selected the rest of his equipment accordingly. She did not give him horns, fangs, or claws to defend himself with, but hands with which to fashion weapons. The meaning of all this seems clear. In giving man reason, nature wished him to produce everything from out of himself. She wanted man "to partake of no other beatitude or perfection than that which he had gained by his own reason, free from instinct." But this is something no individual can do; it can be accomplished only by the human species in the course of its history. Consequently, "the older generations seem to carry on their arduous toil only for the sake of the generations to come. This is necessary once we assume that an animal species is endowed with reason and that this class of rational beings—all of whom must die, while the species is immortal—must nevertheless attain to a perfect development of its dispositions."

Kant further finds "natural purpose" in a teleological causality which reaches out beyond the conscious will of men. At first the instrumentality which develops man's dispositions is not the good will of reason, but a causality which operates regardless of whether the will is good or evil. The struggles of man against man, so repugnant to the good will, social "antagonisms," become the "cause" of a lawful order of society. Man has a tendency to form societies (because it is only in a social state that he feels himself to be a man), but also an inclination to isolate himself (because he also has the asocial trait of wishing to do exactly as he pleases). The result is an asocial society which whets all the powers of man. Driven by ambition, love of power, acquisitiveness, he overcomes his leaning to sloth. He "seeks to acquire a rank among his fellow men, whom he detests, but without whom he cannot live." Without injustice, which gives rise to the resistance of all against all, "men's talents would remain forever latent in an Arcadian, pastoral life, characterized by perfect harmony, self-sufficiency, and mutual love. As gentle as the sheep they feed, men would be scarcely better equipped than these same sheep to give greater value to their existence. And so, thanks be to nature for the disharmony among men, for their insatiable lust for possessions and for power. Man desires harmony, but nature knows better what is good for his race: nature wants discord. Man would like to live in ease and comfort; but nature plunges him into toil and hardship in order that he may discover weapons with which to combat them and by his ingenuity raise himself above them."

The "ultimate purpose of nature" is conceived by Kant as the reason of the good will. But that is not the beginning. Nature produces the good will, but does so by creating situations in which it produces itself. "It seems to have been utterly indifferent to nature whether man lived well; she wished him to make himself worthy of life and well-being." Ultimately, a society formed by passions and lusts is able to transform itself into an ethical body.

These ideas, so simply stated, seem to present a contradiction. Kant seems at every step to progress from nature to freedom and then to make freedom into an instrument of the superior natural purpose. Only if we have learned to think in the Kantian manner can we avoid the misunderstandings that are bound to result from a mechanical interpretation of such texts. For Kant, in his thinking, leaps back and forth between the speculative discovery of a natural purpose and the rising self-consciousness of the good will, between theoretical knowledge and thinking political action, between causality and freedom.

Man can regard history as a natural process or else, standing in it, he can help to produce it out of his own freedom. He gains knowledge of history, and he makes demands on his own freedom. The theory of history treats free action itself as a factor. The appeal to freedom in historical action treats theoretical knowledge as its material or as a means of orientation in the historical situation. The relation between being (process) and the "ought" (freedom) creates an insurmountable tension in the philosophy of history and politics: my theoretical idea is itself a factor in action, hence even in thinking it I bear a responsibility. What I do is dependent on my thinking and is at the same time an object of my thinking. History presents a twofold aspect: on the one hand, process without human planning, natural purpose (Providence); on the other, the spiritual realm of rational beings, the community of consciences.

In his philosophy of history, Kant aims to provide a ground both for the historical, causal explanation and for the appeal to freedom. He does not mix them, though he recognizes that they are inseparable in every significant interpretation of history. But his thinking has two sources. *First,* in line with the *Critique of Teleological Judgment,* he conceives of a natural purposiveness. Through it, he arrives at an objective understanding of the astonishing way in which series of events have balanced and complemented one another. *Second,* he follows out the practical philosophy of freedom, which commands man to do what he himself has recognized to be his duty. This freedom is for Kant the "hypothetical beginning" of history and is represented as a breach with nature. It determines progress.

History, the path between beginning and end, is at once process and free action. Because it is both, man cannot survey the consequences of his action; but neither is he at the mercy of a process that takes place without him. The idea of the goal is itself a factor that drives man toward the goal. The path is a progress, which springs from the freedom of each individual as responsible for his action, but the medium in which it develops consists of partly understandable natural necessities, which are seen as the effects of a hidden purpose, driving toward a goal that is fulfilled through freedom.

E. *Limited aspects of historical knowledge:* The course of human history, says Kant, is no more known to us than the path of the sun in the universe. Generally, seen in the scheme of an Idea, this course moves from an origin to a goal. But the origin can only be constructively conjectured, the goal can only be projected as an Idea. The history that we can observe or investigate lies in between.

In his theoretical philosophy of history, Kant examines history for indications of a course providential to man. He never claims that the "natural purpose" or "Providence" can be definitely known. But he holds the question to be within the prerogatives of reason, which investigates historical reality to see how far the facts correspond to a conjectural design. He does not pretend that any such hypothetical design represents a knowledge of the total process, but recognizes the inadequacy of any total view of history.

I. *Progress:* Kant does not claim that we can be certain of progress as the all-pervading fact of history and predict further progress.

He thinks through three possibilities. *First:* The human race is in continuous regression; things are getting worse and worse, the end is imminent. *Second:* The good is on the increase. But this happens only through freedom and would therefore require a greater store of good than man possesses. *Third:* Things remain as they are. Foolish bustle is the hallmark of the species; man keeps trying to push the boulder of Sisyphus uphill and it keeps rolling back down; for every step forward, he takes a step back, good alternates with evil; the activities of our species on this globe are a mere farce, with no more value than those of the other animal species, except that the animals manage with less expenditure of effort and brain power.

Among these three possibilities, says Kant, there can be no empirical choice. Even if observation should indicate a long period of progress, this very day might perfectly well be the turning point that will usher in an era of regression. Observation of a particular period proves nothing for the whole.

Progress can have no bearing on good and evil, for good and evil are not substances that increase or decrease in quantity. The good is always possible for every man. Actions of freedom are not natural events and cannot be predicted like natural events. Insofar as it comes within our field of observation, the progress of mankind can be a progress only of objectively good actions, not of conscience; of legality, not of morality; of civil institutions, not of human worth.

Even though there can be no empirical certainty in regard to progress as a whole, nevertheless the Idea of progress, as a regulative principle, is of practical importance for our freedom—in the Idea of civil order, for example. I cannot know what will be, but I can foresee what I will help to produce. The Idea of progress gives no answer to the question of what will be, but it does tell me what I am aiming at. Under the guidance of the Ideas, the will can act. The Ideas are demonstrated by no previous experience, but they lead to realizations which become an object of experience.

The Idea of progress, not as a content of knowledge, but remaining, as far as we can know, at the crossroads of the three possibilities, is a practical Idea which opens the way to the independence of the good will. Even without adequate knowledge, the good will is justified in regarding itself as a contributory factor on the way to political betterment. It has no call to abandon the possibility of accomplishing something in this world and, vaulting over the world as it were, to seek repose in the postulate of a supertemporal immortality.

When we consider the course of the world and "enumerate the evils," we may easily find fault with Providence. But uncertainty as to whether "the human race may hope for improvement" cannot impair the will. The feeling that there is a "natural purpose" or "Providence" brings us no known certainty, but it fortifies our confidence, regardless of the trials and tribulations that may be in store for the world.

2. *Our standpoint and the standpoint of Providence:* In his conjectural view of the course of history, Kant declares "that in the play of human freedom nature herself does not operate without plan and ultimate aim, but reaches out beyond all human, finite purposes and takes them into her overall plan." He suggests schematically what the plan of Providence might be. However, he makes it very clear that though in our speculation we try to look at things from the standpoint of Providence, this standpoint is not really possible for us. We cannot concretely survey the totality that lies open to the eyes of Providence, but can only elucidate it ad infinitum.

Perhaps the course of events seems "so meaningless" because in judging it we try to take the standpoint of Providence. We cannot reconcile natural causality and freedom. We can tell freely acting beings what they *ought* to do, but we cannot foresee what they *will* do. To Providence, however, free actions, the natural process, and the order of things subordinated to a final purpose are one and the same thing.

3. *Ultimate purpose and final purpose:* In the realm of the Idea, nature and freedom become one as human existence is perfected. But they are not one and cannot be conceived as becoming one in the world. Because perfection is only an Idea and not a possible reality, the world as a whole cannot, like a machine, be perfectly organized according to plan. But because perfection is an Idea, it imposes upon us the task of ordering our particular world as though we were moving closer to perfection. Freedom cuts across time and is itself timeless: the realm of spirits is eternally present where the good will, impelled by conscience, acts ethically and finds itself in a timeless union with all good spirits.

The invisible realm of spirits is a unity that is being realized in the world. Kant terms the highest good in this realm the "final purpose." As to the good which is forever sought in historical time, the goal of a process of perfection guided by the Idea, he calls it the "ultimate purpose." The highest good, "the existence of rational beings under moral laws" and the corresponding state of beatitude—these are possible only under the rule of a supreme Being. This final purpose is a postulate of our practical reason and can be attained only through the Idea of immortality.

In the world, however, there is no final purpose, but only an "ultimate purpose." It is "what should be furthered in man through nature." The ultimate purpose is either a purpose that can be attained through nature: happiness; or else it is "fitness and skill for all manner of purposes," that is, culture. This last is the "ultimate purpose" of man in nature.

But the "ultimate purpose" leaves us dissatisfied. For the question always remains: To what end? It is a question that can arise only in connection with man as a rational, an ethical being. Without man as a rational being, "all creation would be a mere desert, gratuitous and without final purpose." "What man himself must do in order to become a final purpose is distinct from everything that is achieved by nature and its ultimate purpose, culture."

Man's ultimate purpose is not his final purpose. History is subordinated to a higher condition. Or in other words: The whole historical process, in itself imperfectible, cannot be man's final purpose. Or: History is not God.

The final purpose does not lie in the future, for it is supersensible and therefore not subject to temporal conditions. Its place is the actuality of the good will. We represent it in the image of the future, but this future has no objective reality. The "ultimate purpose," however, is happiness in the world. It is infinite and impossible.

Happiness in the world is the material of the world-experience in which the good will takes on reality. In becoming the material of the good will, happiness is transposed to the realm of the supersensible and eternal and ceases to be mere happiness. It is no longer the ultimate purpose but the final purpose.

Kant developed the fundamental ideas of his view of history in concrete aspects: *first,* in his construction of the Idea of a "civil society"; *second,* in his view of enlightenment as the way to attain to it; *third,* in his view of his own epoch.

2. *The Idea of Civil Society*

To establish, preserve, and develop a civil society is the highest task of the human race.

The genesis of society can neither be observed nor represented. Man does not precede society. "At the creation of states as at the creation of the world, no man was present, for to be present a man would have had to be his own Creator." But the state is not perfect. The perfection of the state is a dream, a task.

A. *The "republican" order:* In a civil society, the greatest freedom—and consequently a thoroughgoing antagonism among its members—should be combined with an exact definition of the limits of this freedom. One man's freedom must extend only as far as compatible with the freedom of the others. This limitation of freedom is made possible only by law, behind which stands a power which, itself guided by legality, sees to it that the law is respected. Hence civil government is a relationship among free men who, however, are subject to legal coercion. Only in a universal condition secured by an order of this kind can the purpose of the human species be attained: the development of all men's aptitudes, "Just as trees in a forest, by trying, each one, to take air and sunlight from the others, compel each other to seek both air and sunlight above them and so achieve a fine, straight growth; while those which freely let their branches grow as they please, develop a stunted, crooked growth. All culture and art, and the best social order, are fruits of unsocial impulses, which compel one another to discipline themselves."

That is the hardest thing to do. If man is an animal who needs a master, it is because he abuses his freedom in regard to his fellow men. He desires a law, but tends "to except himself when he can." A master must curb the individual's will and compel him to obey the universal will. But the master in turn will always be a man, and so each master will abuse his freedom, unless there stands over him another master endowed with power. The supreme master ought to be just, but he again is only a man. A perfect solution to this problem is impossible. "From such crooked wood as that which man is made of nothing straight can be fashioned." The ideal, however, is a just sovereignty with the power to enforce its will, and it is our duty to do our utmost toward realizing that ideal. In practice, freedom and law must go hand in hand. The state must have power to enforce the law against the abuse of freedom. Where this is the case, Kant speaks of a "republican" order. Law and freedom without power signify "anarchy"; law and power without freedom mean "despotism"; power without freedom and law characterizes "barbarism."

Only the republican order deserves the name of a civil government. Here the citizens are subject to laws which they themselves have made and which derive authority and stability from an irresistible power. "The best order is one in which the power stems not from men but from laws." The obligation to preserve such an order, once it exists, is the supreme law of a civil society.

Kant judges societies, not by their *form* of government—monarchy, aristocracy, or democracy—but rather by their mode of government—republican, despotic, or barbaric. "The mode of government is incomparably more important for a nation than the form of state." The mode of government is the constitutional order. In Kant's view, a monarchy may be republican, while a democracy may be despotic, and conversely. The notion of a constitution implies that "those who obey the law should at the same time, united in a body, be the legislators." That is "the eternal norm for all civil government."

The republican order has as its principle the separation of the executive from the legislative power. In a despotism, on the other hand, the government autocratically executes laws it has also made. "Democracy in the strict sense is necessarily a despotism." For it implies an executive power "in which all make decisions about a single member, if not against him, so that it is all, and yet not all, who do the deciding." The universal will is in conflict with itself and with freedom. But in another sense Kant says: "All civil government is fundamentally democratic," that is to say, the people govern in a form characterized by the separation of powers (legislative, executive, judiciary).

Republican government of this kind requires the representative system. Without it, there can only be despotism. "None of the ancient so-called republics knew this and inevitably they degenerated into despotism." "Any form of government that is not representative is a monstrosity, because the legislator in person can be the executor of his own will."

B. *Happiness and law:* In a republican order, "each man pursues his own happiness and every citizen is free to enter into dealings with every other citizen. It is not the function of government to relieve the private person of this concern." The determining principle of a republican society is not happiness but right (justice). The principle of right is conceived as a social contract. The "public is equivalent to the legal constitution which, by means of laws, secures the freedom of every man."

A civil society cannot be grounded on "men's ever varying notion of what constitutes their happiness." In such a society, rather, each man is free to form his own conception of his happiness. The government has no right to make men happy against their will, but must merely see to it that the people live together as a community. "Where the supreme power hands down laws that are primarily directed toward happiness (prosperity, etc.), happiness is not viewed as an end, but as a means of safeguarding the legal state of affairs, particularly against external enemies."

The principle of right is unconditional within the state. As to the principle of happiness, first, it is no principle at all. But second and more important, if it is substituted for the principle of right, it foments political and moral evil. Even if the principle of happiness is put forward in good faith, its consequences are disastrous both for the ruler and the ruled: "The sovereign wishes to make the people happy in his own way and becomes a despot; the people are unwilling to forgo the universal human claim to determine their own happiness and become rebellious."

c. *Tyranny and rebellion:* Kant examines illegality and its consequences.

First on the part of the people: rebellion is the worst of crimes, because it destroys the foundations of the supreme legislative power. The prohibition of rebellion is absolute. If the right to resist authority were raised to the level of a maxim, all legal government would become uncertain and law itself would be annulled. For in connection with a rebellion no one can decide on what side the right lies. Neither party can be a judge in his own cause. There is no higher authority.

Indispensable to the life of the state, the principle of right is binding on the sovereign as well as the people. Hobbes had said that the sovereign was in no way obligated by his original contract with the people. Kant takes the contrary view. The people "likewise have their irreducible rights over against those of the sovereign, although these cannot be enforced." Here is the crucial point. Hobbes's principle would be "correct if by injustice we meant an offense which gave the offended party a right to exert coercion against the offender." But taken universally, Hobbes's principle "is an abomination." For it denies the rights of the people.

Then the people have a right which, unlike all other right, is secured by no power of coercion. But what if—since according to Kant the rulers are only men—they infringe on this right to the extent of annulling it? Kant replies:

In every state, obedience to coercive laws must go hand in hand with the "spirit of freedom." Where the spirit of freedom prevails, "my reason convinces me that the coercion is just."

An obedient subject must be able to assume that his sovereign did not wish to wrong him, that the injustice has sprung solely from "error or ignorance." Accordingly, the citizen, with the sovereign's consent, must be entitled to express his opinion about any of the sovereign's acts that he may regard as hostile to the common weal.

To be incapable of error and ignorance, a sovereign would have to be divinely inspired and superhuman. Thus freedom of the pen is the palladium of the people's right. To suppress it (according to Hobbes) is to deprive the people of all claim to just treatment at the hands of the supreme power, and to deprive the sovereign of all knowledge of evils that he would modify were he aware of them.

The principle governing this right to judge the measures and laws of the government is: "What the people cannot decide in regard to themselves, the legislator cannot decide for them."

It is right, legality, that makes it possible for men to live together in a community. But a perfect state of legality can never be achieved. Tyranny can carry law to the point of lawlessness. Rebellion can threaten its existence. The people have no right that can justify disobedience and violent revolution. The sovereign has no right that can justify him in setting aside the law. Both ought to obey. Kant holds that rebellion and tyranny, like war, imperil the community as a whole. There is no adequate justification for them. Such actions are not based on the principle of right. Here natural causality and perhaps Providence make decisions that man can never fully understand. The principle of right is suspended, and there is no longer a lawful authority. Men call on Heaven to pronounce its verdict or simply put their trust in naked force. There remains something which cannot be justified by law, but which actually makes possible a lawful state of affairs. "Once a revolution has been successful and a new order established," says Kant, "the illegality of the beginning cannot free the subjects from the obligation to bow as good citizens to the new order of things."

In case of conflict, the government may choose between two principles as a basis of its decisions: the principle of right and the principle of practical human experience. Either there is a constitutional law that has binding authority quite apart from the well-being of the citizens; then there is also "a theory of constitutional law and no practice that does not accord with it can be valid." Or else there are only men with their passions and their passivity, who have grown accustomed to a certain state of affairs. Although they have notions of right, they are incapable and unworthy of being treated in accordance with them. Then there is no theory of right, but only a practice of governing, based on experience. A "supreme power which operates merely in accordance with rules of expedience" may and must keep men in a state of order and submission.

These, says Kant, are counsels of despair. But where they are followed, "when right gives way to might, the people may attempt to exert force of their own and so imperil all legal government." And "unless there is something [e.g., the principle of human right] which commands immediate respect through reason, all influences are powerless" to check human arbitrariness. But "when right speaks aloud, human nature is sufficiently uncorrupted to hear its voice with veneration."

Kant demands that the claims of civil government be recognized in their greatness and harshness. He speaks of right primarily and of the other motivation of history only in discussing the limits of right. But there is another force, Providence or natural purpose, which can bring forth progress from evil or catastrophe. That is why the question of war and peace occupies a central position in Kant's political thinking.

D. *War and peace:* War is the greatest of evils. On the material side: devastation, economic ruin resulting from the constant increase of armaments in peacetime and from the burden of debt after the war. On the ethical side: "the corruption of morals," "the destruction of everything that is good," "the greatest of obstacles to morality." Freedom itself is impaired. External dangers are invoked to justify measures of constraint.

But Kant also says something very different that would seem to contradict the above. From the broad historical standpoint, he finds a natural purpose in war. "War, so great an evil as it is, is also the motive that leads men to exchange the raw state of nature for a civil state." And this is true even today: "At the stage of culture where the human race still stands, war is an indispensable means of progress, and only when culture has been perfected (Heaven knows when!) will an everlasting peace be beneficial to us or even possible." The antagonism of forces exists in order to destroy "mere worthless existence" as well as "sordid luxury," because they rest on a false foundation. Where the state of lawful freedom is not truly grounded in morality, war discloses the flaw. Society harvests the fruits of its actions, of its way of life. If it is not to succumb, it must perceive the meaning of its disastrous state, let necessity drive it to the Idea of its task, and so advance in ethical freedom.

After such arguments, a reader may suppose that it is only a step to the glorification of war, or worse, if the following sentences from the "Critique of Aesthetic Judgment" are taken into account:

For what is that which is, even to the savage, an object of the greatest admiration? It is a man who shrinks from nothing, who fears nothing, and therefore does not yield to danger, but rather goes to face it vigorously with the most complete deliberation. Even in the most highly civilized state this peculiar veneration for the soldier remains, though only under the condition that he exhibit all the virtues of peace, gentleness, compassion, and even a becoming care for his own person; because even by these it is recognized that his mind is unsubdued by danger. Hence whatever disputes there may be about the superiority of the respect which is to be accorded them, in the comparison of a statesman and a general, the aesthetical judgment decides for the latter. War itself, if it is carried on with order and with a sacred respect for the rights of citizens, has something sublime in it, and makes the disposition of the people who carry it on thus only the more sublime, the more numerous are the dangers to which they are exposed and in respect of which they behave with courage. On the other hand, a long peace generally brings about a predominant commercial spirit and, along with it, low selfishness, cowardice, and effeminacy, and debases the disposition of the people.

Thus war provides an occasion on which man's character can rise above the circumstances of his life, but it is not war that produces such sublimity. Kant does not regard the soldier's life as great in itself; he is a far cry from the militarist for whom war exerts a magic charm, who sees man's highest purpose in a soldier's death, and heroism in power as such. "We should cease," he says, "to hold military theory in high esteem and consider it a vital factor in history, except where it has in some way furthered the progress of the human race." In Kant's opinion Caesar's art of war did nothing for human progress. "Caesar was a wrong-thinking prince, not because he took power, but because, when he had the power, he did not subordinate himself to a rationally ordered commonwealth."

But if war is a part of the natural purpose (Providence) and if we have not yet reached the stage of ethical development that makes war impossible and unnecessary, should we not desire it as a means of furthering the natural purpose as a whole? All Kant's thinking takes the opposite direction, toward eternal peace as the regulative principle which it is our duty to follow in political action and in all ethical existence both public and private. One can accuse Kant of justifying war only by supposing that he meant his speculative constructions in regard to natural purpose as foundations of human planning. But though man may speculate concerning the designs of Providence, his point of view cannot be that of Providence. He cannot act as an agent of Providence but only as a man.

It is our rational duty to pursue the Idea of eternal peace. "Reason absolutely condemns war as a legal procedure." The question is "not whether eternal peace is a reality or a chimera; we must act as though it were a reality" and work toward the order best suited to bring it about, to put an end to ruinous warfare. The speculative constructions of natural purpose or Providence serve to elucidate the indispensable conditions of peace. Kant shows that these conditions are unyielding. If they are not fulfilled, war is a certainty. And if war is certain, the speculative insight becomes a mere reminder to men that perhaps the horrors of war are included in the designs of Providence. It does not detract from the ethical striving to create the conditions that will make war impossible. War cannot simply be abolished. We must transform man's character in such a way as to make war impossible. Kant derives two trains of thought from the Idea of eternal peace.

(1) Natural purpose implies a need that will compel its accomplishment. Just as the struggle of all against all compelled men to form a civil society, so the constant threat of real wars must compel states to associate. The step taken by free, undisciplined men must be repeated by the free undisciplined states.

(2) But, on the other hand, Kant sees that natural purpose does not operate automatically, but only through human freedom. The conditions of peace must become clear to all the citizens. In his book *On Eternal Peace,* Kant formulates those conditions with an earnestness that sometimes takes the form of playful irony. He states them, succinctly, in terms of the peace treaties of his time, which consisted of "preliminary articles," "definitive

articles," and "secret articles." Among the preliminary articles: "No state at war with another state should engage in hostilities of such a kind as to render mutual confidence impossible when peace will have been made."

Among the definitive articles, one is crucial: "The civil order in every state should be republican." Kant perceived the relation between the social order and the conduct of foreign affairs. The conditions necessary for a genuine will to peace are possible only in a state characterized by lawful freedom.

Does it follow that the republican constitution should be imposed on all peoples by coercion? One article reads: "No state should interfere in the constitution and government of another state." For international law can be based only on a federation of free states. But this applies only to states that already have a civil constitution, which alone can provide the required security. A state without a civil (republican) constitution is a threat to other states (just as one individual menaces another in the state of nature). By its mere presence beside us, it threatens us with the lawlessness of its condition.

Universal peace can be guaranteed only by a system of law which joins all states and which is backed by a power that guarantees the observance of its laws (the treaties) by the possibility of coercion. Kant knew that the Idea of eternal peace is an "Idea." We cannot tell whether he thought the Idea could ever be fully realized, but it is perfectly clear that he believed an "approach to the Idea" to be perfectly possible and the duty of rational beings. He examines the vast difficulties, and makes a number of suggestions that cannot lay claim to absolute validity.

International law is shown to be of questionable value as long as there is no supreme authority to enforce it. There is no room in international law for a "right to wage war." If a nation says: Let there be no war between us, for we ourselves will appoint a supreme legislative, executive, and judiciary power that will peacefully arbitrate any disputes between us, that is comprehensible. But if the same state says: Let there be no war between me and other states, although I recognize no supreme legislative power to guarantee my rights and those of other states—it is impossible to see what ground I have for confidence.

The states obstruct the realization of the Idea by their insistence on sovereignty. Just as in establishing civil society, men preferred the rational freedom of the lawful order to the wild freedom of savages, one might think that states would be eager to abandon the lawless violence of the crude natural condition. But instead, every state sees its sovereignty as freedom from all outward constraint. In the free relations among peoples, the wickedness of human nature stands naked before our eyes. Within civil society, it is veiled by the constraint of the government. Thus, in all honesty, we should banish the word "right" from all discussion of war. But so far no state has been so bold as to advocate such a measure. For

"Hugo Grotius, Pufendorf, etc. (all of them poor comforters) are still faithfully invoked in justification of military aggression," although their code of law cannot have the slightest legal force, because states as such are not subject to a common outward constraint. Arguments citing these authorities have never moved any state to desist from its intentions. But the respect for the concept of right, which every state expresses at least in words, proves that man has a latent moral disposition which may someday come to master the evil principle in him.

The right of each state can be safeguarded only by "a surrogate of the civil covenant, namely a free federalism." Kant has in mind a special form of alliance, a league of nations, which would aim not to increase the power of any state, but solely to safeguard the freedom of all the allied states, though there would be no laws providing for coercion. A peace pact of this sort would differ from a peace treaty. It would aim to end not merely one war, but all wars. It would not be the positive ideal of a world republic, but only a substitute, a negative league against war, always subject to an eruption of warlike inclinations.

We cannot record Kant's ideas on the federative state, the league of nations, the alliance between states, and the peace treaty. Kant neither predicts how the Idea of eternal peace will lead to concrete accomplishments nor gives a clear program (which in any case could be only the schema of the Idea, not an account of its realization). Kant has in mind a federalism rather than a world state, chiefly because "excessively large states, as has been witnessed on a number of occasions, can become still more dangerous to freedom by fostering the most terrible despotism." Perhaps this federalism will emanate from a center: "For if fortune decrees that a powerful and enlightened people should form a republic (which by nature must incline toward eternal peace), this republic will provide a center of federative union, which other states will join with a view to safeguarding the freedom of all in accordance with the Idea of international law. Little by little, through several unions of this kind, the federative idea will spread."

Kant never draws up a definite program for world peace, and this may be ascribed to the earnestness and depth of his political thinking: Cosmopolitan society is an Idea. Because it is unattainable, it is not a constitutive, but a regulative principle. That is to say: we should pursue it with all our strength as the mission of the human race, and we are even entitled to presume that we shall be helped by a *natural* tendency in that direction.

Kant refers to the Abbé de Saint-Pierre, who in 1714, after the War of the Spanish Succession, wrote his famous treatise on eternal peace, ridiculed at the time as utopian. But the difference is radical. The Abbé projected an organization of princes; his system is based on their good will. Kant has in mind the will of the peoples; he presupposes a "republican" constitution and draws his inferences from necessity. The Abbé draws up a program that the princes are supposed to accept. Kant outlines a path on which the ethical imperative coincides with natural necessity. The Abbé wishes to establish eternal peace at one stroke. Kant, within the framework of his philosophy of history, works out the presuppositions of eternal peace.

In Kant's view, the development from the natural state of war to a state of peace among all men takes place in stages. In the first stage, a legal order is established in each country; in the second, international law governs the relations between states; the third and final stage is characterized by a cosmopolitan order in which men and states would be looked upon as citizens of a universal state embracing all mankind.

Kant develops this notion of world citizenship only in one point. Men cannot disperse indefinitely, because the surface of the earth is limited. They must suffer other men to live beside them and use their land rights as a possible basis for commerce. This presupposes the right of hospitality, which provides a basis for intercourse and commerce between natives and newcomers. These in turn foster peaceful relations which ultimately are formulated in terms of law. Thus a step is taken toward a cosmopolitan order of the human race.

Kant condemns the inhospitality of the commercial states of our continent, the colonial exploitation: "They counted the natives for nothing." But since community between the peoples of the earth has advanced to the point where an injustice at one point in the world is felt everywhere, the idea of a cosmopolitan law is not fantastic. International relations stand indeed in need of an international law and can no longer be safely left to the observance of an unwritten code in international relations. Neither human rights nor eternal peace can be safeguarded in any other way.

E. *The importance of a philosophy of history for human action:* Let us not misunderstand Kant. He does not contend that because war may possibly act as an instrument of the natural purpose, a man can be justified in desiring it.

Kant speculatively constructs a natural purpose which utilizes the acts of the human will, good and evil alike, to attain an end that no human plan provides for. The natural purpose as a whole cannot be made into a human plan because the standpoint of Providence is not that of man.

However, Kant's constructions of a natural purpose are of two kinds. Some are "schemata of the Idea" by which we should be guided (e.g., "republican order," "eternal peace"). Let us suppose that unbeknown to man, history works toward such goals. If this is so, the discovery in history of any traces of natural purpose, however uncertain, will surely be a benefit to mankind. For then it follows "that through our own rational conduct we may hasten the coming of a moment that will be so gratifying to those who come after us."

Kant does not believe that history gives us the experience from which we derive a knowledge of what should be done. On the contrary: in respect to the ought, experience proves nothing that reason does not know by itself. Reason enjoins itself to realize an Idea which no previous experience can demonstrate but which only in its realization becomes an object of experience.

Others are constructions of the means employed by Providence. They do not provide knowledge of real events, hence they cannot, like our cognitions concerning nature, be employed for technical ends. We men are forces which participate in the natural purpose through what we ought to do and even through what we ought not to do.

Kant's natural purpose implies a knowledge of the whole, and we cannot lay claim to any such knowledge. It is only by radically deluding ourselves that we can base a human plan on a natural purpose which we supposedly discern in the whole. If we had to know the whole in order to do what is right in the particular instance, we should never do anything. Must we, in order to act, devise a theory of universal history? We require no such theory (whether demonstrated or demonstrable, probable or improbable) that sets itself up as knowledge. For all alleged knowledge of the whole is pseudo knowledge and can only hamper our efforts at realization. It is precisely by forgoing a knowledge that is not possible that I shall find the right way. Then I shall not claim to know that any particular line of action is right once and for all and, in a spirit of openness, communication with others, willingness to accept correction, I shall let myself be guided by the Ideas which remain forever certain.

Earnestness of action, clarity of judgment here and now, the uncompromising demand of the Idea—these are the lessons of free speculation in the philosophy of history.

It would be absurd on our part to attempt, as though playing the part of Providence, to carry out what we regard as the possible purpose of nature. Our will is subject to the limitation that we can never know the whole. Only "from Providence can we expect a successful outcome which encompasses the whole and thence carries to the parts." But the plans of man "always start from the parts." They remain confined to the parts, "and as for the whole, which is too large for them, they can extend their Idea to it but not their influence."

Providence (according to the human construction) has employed both good and evil as means to its end. But we may not employ evil as a means. For us, insofar as we are rational and therefore moral beings, all planning, all striving for power is subject to the standard of the ethical imperative. Kant's philosophy goes counter to the totalizations that began with the systems of German idealism and led by way of Marxism to the practice of total knowledge and total planning.

What significance has insight into the philosophy of history if it is not applicable as knowledge? It can make for confidence in political action despite all evil. Kant bids the historian to examine events in the light of their bearing on the movement toward the Idea. "The history of states must be written in such a way as to show what benefit the world has derived from a form of government. The revolutions in Switzerland, Holland, England are the most important events of the late period." But, in addition, Kant advised historians to follow out a hypothetical natural purpose in order to discover the traces that point to it. For where such traces are discovered, Kant holds, they encourage the hope that the natural purpose comes to the help of men's insight and good will and compels the devil himself to serve them.

He finds ground for confidence in the observation that the good seems to produce enduring results. Once it is present, it seems to preserve itself, to become dominant, while evil destroys itself. In the end, to be sure, everything is destroyed by natural catastrophes. But within the natural process, the good, which cuts across time and is rooted in the supersensible, seems to have relatively enduring consequences in time.

In Kant, we must distinguish, *first,* the hypothetical constructions of a natural purpose; *second,* the faith in a historical meaning, a faith which springs from ethical sources and is nurtured by indications in experience, but never proved; *third,* the suggestions of institutional possibilities and valid maxims, by which we may seek to realize the Ideas of civil society and eternal peace.

The clarity with which Kant discloses the tension between nature and freedom, between "is" and "ought," forbids us to make an amalgam of these lines of thought.

3. *The Way of Enlightenment*

Kant sees our historic existence as a small part of a process whose beginning and end are not accessible to experience. The beginning can be conjectured, the necessary Ideas may give an indication of the direction in which the goal lies. The actual way to it is the process of enlightenment. "Enlightenment is man's exodus from the state of tutelage for which he himself is to blame." By "tutelage" Kant means inability to use his own mind without guidance from without. Man is to blame for it because of his lack of courage, his irresoluteness and preference for easy solutions. The motto of enlightenment is: *Sapere aude.* Have the courage to use your own mind.

Many men are glad to live in a state of tutelage. A book furnishes them with "'intelligence," a spiritual guide provides them with a "conscience," a physician chooses their "diet" for them—and thus all effort is spared them. Their guardians, who have kindly undertaken the task of managing their affairs, take care of them and for greater security keep them in chains. Most men fear the step to majority. Precepts and formulas are their chains. If the chains were taken away, they would still be unable to walk, because they are not accustomed to free movement. Yet enlightenment makes its way. Casting off their own chains, a few original thinkers divulge the spirit of independent thought and teach men a rational estimation of their own worth. The spread of enlightenment is inevitable but slow. A revolution may cast off a personal despotism but can never bring about a true reform in men's way of thinking. New prejudices take the place of the old, for ways of thinking do not change suddenly.

Kant's passion for rational thought is his philosophy itself, with which he knew himself to be participating in a great historical movement. His philosophy is political, because he wants thought to be an element of politics. His political thought is philosophical, because it is bound to free reason and hence to the experience of transcending. His political thinking is fraught with the tension between awareness of momentary helplessness and a vast confidence inspired by the signs of reason's progress.

The role of philosophy in political life is implicit in Kant's conception of philosophy.

A. *The role of philosophy:* According to Kant, the role of philosophers in the community is not to act but to give counsel. He does not (with Plato) expect kings to be philosophers or philosophers kings; he does not even think it desirable, "because the possession of power inevitably obstructs the free judgment of reason." But kings or kingly peoples (those who govern themselves according to laws of equality) should hearken to the philosophers, because the counsel of the philosophers is indispensable to the conduct of the state's affairs. They must not reduce the philosophers to silence. Kant included the following "secret article" in his charter of eternal peace: "States preparing for war should consult the maxims of the philosophers relating to the conditions under which peace is possible among nations." Why secret? Because it might "seem humiliating for the authority to ask his subjects [the philosophers] for advice." Accordingly, the article demands merely that they be permitted to speak. In the hierarchy of power, the philosophers are below the jurists and theologians. That is why philosophy was formerly called the "handmaiden of theology." "But it is hard to see whether she bears the torch in advance of her gracious lady or carries her train behind her."

The distinction of the philosophers is that by the very nature of their occupation they do not form cliques and clubs, that they are not a class or corporation; consequently, they wield no power. They counsel the people, "not according to agreements made among themselves (like a clergy) but as fellow citizens." They "make it indubitably clear that their concern is for the truth." The people are interested "because of a general feeling that their moral aptitudes are in need of cultivation." Hence it is advisable in a body politic to lend ear "not only to the traditional pious doctrines, but also to practical reason as elucidated by philosophy," that is to say, to accord freedom to "those who are wise (after the manner of men)."

These ideas concerning the place of philosophy in the community, which Kant sets forth ironically but in deep earnestness, only become fully understandable when we know Kant's view of the essence of philosophy. This he tells us with a magnificent simplicity.

1. *"You can never learn philosophy, but at most how to philosophize."*

By this Kant means that though we can learn a philosophy as a scholar learns historic data, historical knowledge of a philosophy gives no indication of an independent judgment based on insight. We have "molded ourselves to another man's reason," we are "a plaster cast," we judge only as much as was given. Accordingly, anyone who wishes not merely to gather historical learning about philosophy, but to philosophize on his own account, must "regard all systems as no more than a history of the use of reason," and use them only as material for exercise.

Kant expressed these ideas as early as 1765. What a student should learn is not ideas but how to think. "The young man who has just completed his secondary schooling has been in the habit of learning. And now, he thinks, he will learn philosophy. But that is impossible; what he must learn is how to philosophize." He can learn the historical and mathematical sciences, which to a certain degree are set before us as finished disciplines. The notion of "learning philosophy" presupposes the existence of a complete philosophy. "It would have to be possible to take a book from the shelves and say: Behold, here is wisdom and reliable insight." A teacher would be untrue to his mission if, "instead of trying to broaden the mental faculties of the young men entrusted to him, instead of training them to develop independent insights, he should deceive them by pretending to possess a finished philosophy."

Still Kant's aim is the *one* philosophy, "the system of all philosophical knowledge." By this he means objectively "the archetype by which to judge all attempts at philosophizing." "Thus philosophy becomes a mere Idea of a possible science, which is nowhere given *in concreto*." We approach it by many different ways, "until the one path, very much overgrown with sensibility, is discovered." And Kant was convinced that he had discovered the one path and was approaching the archetype of philosophy. He went so far as to say that "before the critical philosophy came into being, there was no philosophy. Before we can pass sentence on so seemingly presumptuous a remark, we must ask: Can there be more than one philosophy?" There have been different ways of philosophizing.

Many attempts of this kind had to be made—and each one of them made its contribution to the present philosophy—but since, objectively considered, there can be only one human reason, there cannot be many philosophies, that is to say, only one true system of philosophy derived from principles is possible. . . . And so, to represent a system of philosophy as of one's own making is tantamount to saying: before this philosophy there was no other. . . . Consequently, if I represent the critical philosophy as a philosophy prior to which there was nowhere any philosophy at all, I am only doing what all those who devise a philosophy according to a plan of their own have done, will do, and indeed must do.

2. Kant distinguishes between philosophy in the academic sense and philosophy as it is understood by the world at large, world philosophy.

Academic philosophy is "a system of knowledge that is no more than a science. It has no higher aim than logical completeness. One who philosophizes in this academic sense is a mere acrobat of reason, a philo-dox, a lover of opinion, rather than a philo-sopher, a lover of wisdom. He strives merely for speculative knowledge, making no attempt to find out how much his knowledge contributes to the ultimate purpose of human reason. He hands down rules by which reason can be applied to all manner of ends; he teaches logical gymnastics. But there is always a world philosophy underlying academic philosophy. World philosophy is "the science dealing with the relation of all knowledge to the essential aims of human reason, and the philosopher is not an intellectual acrobat but the legislator of human reason." Only this lofty conception can "lend dignity, i.e., an absolute value, to philosophy."

Our many purposes are not the highest purpose. There can only be one final purpose. It is "the whole aim of mankind, and the philosophy that deals with it is called ethics." For the ancients, accordingly, the word "philosopher" meant, "also and eminently, a moralist." When a man, however unlearned, presents even "the outward appearance of self-mastery through reason," we still tend, according to a certain analogy, to call him a philosopher.

World philosophy is the philosophy that "concerns all men." It "does not surpass the common understanding" and it is "not discovered only by philosophers." In regard to what concerns all men without distinction, nature has distributed her gifts impartially, "and in regard to the essential purposes of human nature, the highest philosophy cannot surpass the guidance nature herself has imparted to the commonest of minds."

In 1781, Kant devised "a plan for popularizing his total revolution in thinking," his "metaphysic of metaphysics." "For," he wrote in 1783, "every philosophical work must be susceptible of popularity; if not, it probably conceals nonsense beneath a fog of seeming sophistication." Later, however (1796), Kant, though still professing "that it must be possible to popularize any philosophical doctrine," makes an exception for his critical system: "No more than any other formal system of metaphysics, can it ever be popularized, although the conclusions can be made perfectly clear to the sound reason (of any man who is a metaphysician without knowing it)." In dealing with metaphysics, one is driven to "scholastic punctilio," to "school language," "because there is no other way to make the over-hasty reason understand itself before it proceeds to make dogmatic assertions."

3. The philosophy which combines worldly wisdom and school philosophy is a *scientific doctrine of wisdom*. This is the lofty meaning the ancients gave the word. Philosophy is the science which shows "what is to be recognized as the highest good and the conduct by which it is to be gained." It would be well, says Kant, to employ the word in its old meaning. Philosophy is then "a doctrine of the highest good insofar as reason strives

to raise this doctrine to the level of a science." For "science is the strait gate that leads to a doctrine of wisdom." Science without wisdom is meaningless, wisdom without science is unreal.

Science can chart "the way to wisdom that every man should travel" and save us from going astray. This science is at all times taken into philosophy, in whose "subtle investigations the public has no part, but in whose teachings it should share." The sciences by themselves are of questionable value, because they do not provide their own ground of truth. Philosophy alone has "dignity, that is, an intrinsic, absolute value." It is philosophy that gives value to all other knowledge. "For only as an organ of wisdom has science a true intrinsic value." Because only philosophy provides the sciences with a systematic order, it may be said to close the scientific circle.

4. Kant's critical philosophy was looked upon as destructive by the academic philosophers of his time. His answer was that only the schools were affected by the loss. Yes, the contribution of the scientific philosophy was negative in regard to the speculative use of an erring, self-deluded reason. But by marking off limits (the "discipline of pure reason"), it freed thought from all manner of phantasms *in order to make room for the positive*. It opened the way not only to the sure progress of science but also to faith, a faith grounded in reason. For dogmatism always leads ultimately to skepticism and unbelief, while critique leads to science and faith.

The critical philosophy does not claim to be the whole of philosophy. Kant characterized it with great humility: "Thus, no doubt, the greatest and perhaps the sole contribution of the philosophy of pure reason is negative; for it serves not as an organon for the amplification of knowledge but as a discipline for the definition of limits; it does not discover truth, but has only the modest distinction of averting error."

5. The negative aspect of the critical philosophy is only a factor in philosophy as a whole. Mathematicians, natural scientists, logicians are "after all mere acrobats of reason." "Beyond them, there is a teacher of the ideal, who employs them all, uses them as instruments, in order to further the essential purposes of human reason. It is he alone that we should call a philosopher."

But: "If the word is taken in this sense, it would be vainglorious indeed to call oneself a philosopher and claim to have equaled the archetype which lies only in the Idea." Kant strives to discourage such "self-conceit" by defining the standard. To be a "teacher of wisdom" would mean to embody the mastery of wisdom. But philosophy as wisdom remains an ideal. "Only he is justified in laying claim to it and in calling himself a philosopher who can in his person exemplify the unfailing influence of the ideal (by his self-mastery and his unquestioned concern for the universal good). This is what the ancients expected of those who aspired to the honor of being called philosophers." "The true philosopher is the practical philosopher, who teaches wisdom by doctrine and example."

B. *Publicity:* Philosophers can give counsel only when the rulers do not prohibit or censor free speech. Kant describes the political conditions under which philosophical thinking can be effective.

Publicity is crucial for the life of the community, because communicability and unrestricted communication are the essence of reason. Philosophy understands and engenders the will to communicate. Without the air of communication reason is stifled.

Communicability is essential to all forms of reason. Concepts are communicable, not feelings. The judgment of an ethical action can be "universally communicated through definite concepts of practical reason." The judgment of the beautiful is effected without a concept; the "judgment of taste" implies "the Idea of a common sense," and thus appeals "as it were to the judgment of all reasonable human beings."

Only through communication can reason be amplified and verified. Communication is the indispensable condition of humanity. Humanity consists in "communicability." In observing the function of taste in social culture, Kant declares that "feelings are valued only insofar as they can be communicated to all; then, even though the pleasure may be inconsiderable, the Idea of its universal communicability increases its value almost beyond measure."

"Think for yourself," says Kant in his "Maxims of Common Sense." "Think in harmony with yourself." And he adds: "In your thinking, put yourself in the place of every other man." This is the principle of the "broader thinking" which can go beyond "the private, subjective conditions of judgment."

Freedom of communication is indispensable to freedom of thought. Without communication, thought is restricted to the narrow confines of the individual and open to subjective error. "The external power that deprives man of the freedom to communicate his thoughts, deprives him at the same time of his freedom to think." But freedom of thought must protect itself against the "lawless use of reason," which raises its false claim under the name of genius. "When reason—misled by such claims—refuses to subject itself to the law which it has given *itself,* it must bow beneath the yoke of laws imposed by another; for without a law nothing, not even the greatest absurdity, can long endure." The inevitable consequence of lawlessness in thinking is loss of freedom.

In public life, publicity is the first condition of law. Without it justice cannot be achieved. A citizen must be permitted to publicize all his lawful demands. He is entitled to assume that the sovereign has no wish to do him an injustice. Then any wrong done him must be attributed to error or to a failure to understand all the implications of the laws. It follows that every citizen must be free to publicize his opinion of anything that strikes him as an offense against the common weal. "Consequently, freedom of the pen is the only palladium of people's rights." It is subject only to the restrictions that reason imposes on itself: respect for the political order in which one lives; a liberal attitude. In response to the dictates of public life, writers "impose certain limitations upon themselves lest they lose their freedom."

4. *Kant's View of His Own Age*

In philosophy an era supposedly expresses its self-awareness. But it is only in the last two centuries (after beginnings in antiquity) that philosophers have given express thought to their own time and to the position of their philosophy in it. As the philosopher becomes increasingly aware of his own unconditionality, the understanding of the present becomes for him a will, grounded in history and driving toward the future. He draws the facts of his time into the area of his own responsibility.

Kant's historical consciousness grew hand in hand with the political events of his time. The great turning point was the French Revolution. In the years preceding it Kant had already published articles on the philosophy of history. His manner of thinking enabled him to take a broad view of the event. Political developments now entered the forefront of his thinking; he awaited the news with eagerness, and a new tone became evident in his writing, although he continued to conceive of history and politics in the same antinomies. The French Revolution was to him a sign of the reality of human progress, a philosophical event.

The peace of Basel (1795) was the outward occasion of his book *On Eternal Peace*. His conflict with the ministry over his religious works lay behind him. After the death of Frederick II, he had grown cautious. *On Eternal Peace* begins with a *clausula salvatoria* to the effect that "it would be impossible to detect any danger for the state" in his opinions. The whole is a masterpiece of clear statement despite the pressure to which he was subjected. His profound earnestness is hidden beneath a cloak of irony. He makes his statements "at random," speaks of "dreams," puts his remarks on the importance of philosophical counsel into a "secret article." A further consequence of his caution is that Kant's most important political statements are to be found in his posthumous notes.

We turn to Kant's view of his age.

A. The present age is that of the Enlightenment. That is to say, we are living today, not in an enlightened age, but in an age that is driving toward enlightenment. Yet men are still far from capable of thinking with their own minds. The process of enlightenment requires critique, the testing of the truth through the autonomous operation of reason. "Our age is the age of critique, to which everything must be subjected. Religion would like to evade it on the strength of its sanctity, and legislation on the strength of its majesty. But in so doing they arouse justified suspicions; they cannot lay claim to the undissembled respect which reason accords only to those who can withstand its free and public scrutiny." "Once the tendency to free thought is developed, it will gradually affect the character of the people (who, little by little, become more capable of free action) and in the end will influence the principles of the government."

B. It is an age of absolutism. Consequently, Kant looks to the princes for decisive action. He characterizes the epoch (in 1784) as "the age of enlightenment or the century of Frederick," who made no attempt to regulate religious life and even refused to be called "tolerant" because of the arrogance the term implied. "Reason as much as you will and concerning what you will," he said, "but obey." Herein, Kant sees "a strange, unexpected turn in human affairs; and indeed, when we view the course of history as a whole, almost everything in it seems paradoxical. A higher degree of civil freedom would seem beneficial to the spirit of freedom, and yet sets it insurmountable barriers; a lesser degree, on the other hand, enables the spirit of freedom to develop all its faculties." Here Kant perceived a reality that was to become fully clear only in the following century: that a remarkable amount of intellectual freedom is possible under certain authoritarian regimes (Wilhelminian Germany) and that, as Tocqueville was to observe, democracy could represent a considerable threat to intellectual freedom. Enlightenment, Kant noted, seems to be easy, but it is "difficult, a task that can only be carried out slowly." For the need of reason to legislate for itself can only be readily fulfilled by a truly rational man who, content to perform his essential task, "does not demand to know what surpasses his understanding." The freedom of true reason and political freedom are interdependent.

C. *Evil is still with us:* "Our times are infected with barbarism . . . the honor of princes is still identified with their spirit of heroism. . . . No opprobrium is seen in injustice on the part of a state if it serves the state's aggrandizement. . . . It is generally believed that those who themselves give laws are bound by no laws. Princes have no conception of any rights that may deter them from acting, but speak at best of magnanimity." "There is still something barbaric about states . . . in respect to their neighbors they are unwilling to incur the constraint of any law." "No state does anything for the good of the world, but only for itself."

But a turn is in the offing. What is the present situation? "It is only two centuries ago that we opened up relations with other continents beyond the seas. . . . It is only in the last hundred years that we have known a constitutional system in a great state, England. . . ." "This is the most crucial period, for the energies of the states are for the most part exerted inwardly toward luxury and self-indulgence and externally toward aggression and defense, while armies are larger and more disciplined than ever before. No improvement is possible unless the states take a different form. The courts must accept wisdom from the study halls."

D. Kant expects change and progress from gradual reforms, not from revolutions. For because the population at large remains to be enlightened, nothing salutary can be expected from below. A true republican order, characterized by a separation of powers and representative government, is more possible in a monarchy than in an aristocracy or democracy, "for Frederick II at least *said* that he was no more than the first servant of the state."

Yet despite his conservative, reformist attitude, Kant favored the French Revolution. However—and this is essential—he supported it not because of the immediate practical consequences, not because of its "deeds bad and good," but because of the state of mind manifested in its origins. "The undisguised attitude of the onlookers, the universal, unselfish sympathy they show even at the risk that their partisanship may redound very much to their own disadvantage . . . bear witness to a disposition of the human race as such. That disposition is ethical in germ. It not only gives us a hope of progress, but is in itself a progress." But what was the object of the general enthusiasm? The desire for a republican order, a state based on justice and therefore peaceful. Even if the actual course of events brings failure or takes a turn to tyranny, the progress disclosed at the beginning cannot be annulled. "For a phenomenon of this kind in the history of mankind can never be forgotten."

E. In trying to determine whether the human race as a whole is steadily advancing toward better things, Kant speculates on the possibility of a prophetic history. It is possible, he holds, "if the prophet himself makes and promotes the events he predicts." "Our politicians" say that "men should be taken as they are." They should say, "as we have made them by our unjust exactions and treacherous aggressions, to wit, stubborn and rebellious." In this light, the prophecies of doom emitted by these "supposedly clever statesmen" are true, for if the reins of constraint are relaxed a little, the most unfortunate consequences ensue. Clergymen predict the coming of the Antichrist by doing everything they can to bring it about; instead of urging ethical principles upon their community, they demand observances and traditional belief. They deplore an irreligiosity that they themselves have made.

It would be easier to predict the progressive improvement of the race if we could say that man's will, though limited, is invariably good. For then the prediction would apply to something that man himself can make. "But in view of the mixture in man's disposition of good and evil in proportions of which he is unaware, he himself does not know what to expect."

Nothing can be proved and nothing predicted on the basis of historical experience. But our experience of an event which points to the existence of a cause of improvement, may justify an inference in respect both to the past and the future. Kant regards the French Revolution as a "historical sign" of this sort, indicating the tendency of human history as a whole.

5. Kant's Political Attitude

A. Kant's conception of a history guided by natural purpose seems to imply a "course of events" moving spontaneously toward a rational goal. Man supposes that he is accomplishing of his free will something that is taking place inevitably and all by itself. This is the paradox of the believer, who acts with total conviction because he knows himself to be one with the total process, conceived as Providence, natural purpose, or historical law.

But this is not Kant's attitude. In his construction of a natural purpose, he was attempting to do something of which he himself was unaware. He was attempting, in a sense, to sketch out the designs of Providence, though knowing full well that they are beyond human thinking. For human thinking, as Kant's philosophy has shown by elucidating it down to its very origins, operates on a totally different plane.

But for Kant his constructions were not a mere game, or better still, they were an earnest game, in which he expressed his "satisfaction with Providence and the general course of human affairs, which does not begin with good and move toward evil, but gradually develops from evil toward something better. To this progress, each man is destined by nature itself to contribute his part, as much as is in his power." Kant perceives "the order of a wise Creator, not the hand of a malignant spirit."

B. In order to believe in the meaning of history and take an ethical view of political action, one must *believe in man*. Without such a belief, a mere empirical scrutiny can find only absurdity in the whole.

Belief in man does not mean love of man as he is in reality, but love of the Idea of man. But to love man in his Idea does not mean to love a being who is less or more than man, hence no longer a man, nor does it mean to love the whole reality of each man. Kant has in mind the Idea of man in each man, not a so-called elite and not each individual as such.

Kant asks expressly: "Are we to love the human race as a whole?" Or is it an object that we should regard with distaste, wishing it (lest we seem to be misanthropic) the best of luck, but averting our eyes? His answer is that he rejects "the affectation of universal love of man." Such love can spring only from benevolence, not from affection. For we cannot avoid hating what is evil, not, to be sure, in order to harm people, but in order "to have as little as possible to do with them." As to the human race, we can "love it at least in its steady movement toward the good; otherwise we should have to hate or despise it."

C. Kant himself called attention to the *limits* of his political thinking: the designs of Providence (or of the natural purpose) are impenetrable; we can only speculate concerning them, for in our concrete historical situation we see no fulfillment of any conceivable purpose. Beyond these limits, we are everywhere confronted with mystery. But thanks to the forms of not-knowing that Kant discovered, man can become aware of the mystery through reason.

D. In regard to the nature and aims of political life, the following *principles* may be derived from Kant's philosophizing:

1. Rational politics is concerned only with real situations. It creates the practical conditions under which the aptitudes of man, the components of his freedom, can develop. However, this limitation to the political realm is possible only through absolute moral earnestness. The irresponsibility of wanting too much in politics goes hand in hand with moral corruption. Only the earnestness of ethical reason can avoid confusing questions of practical interest with what is made possible by them and guide us in our dealing with them.

2. Even the greatest of men remains a man and consequently requires control, which can be provided only by reciprocity and openness. Every man has human dignity, but in political action and in the appointment of political orders, which are constantly in need of modification, the evil in all men is a factor to be reckoned with.

3. The medium of political progress is not ethical intentions, but legality. The basic conditions of legality are the observance of contracts and a power, itself regulated by laws, which observes contracts and enforces their observance by others.

4. It is the duty of men to plan rationally, but our knowledge of the limits of knowledge should make us aware of the limitations of rational planning.

E. Kant does not deny the need for experience. Speculative constructions of the whole (philosophy of history) make for an open mind. The experience corresponding to them can never be complete, for temporal human reality, as produced by man himself, is never complete. Living in the world of experience, we orient ourselves and act under the guidance of Ideas. But neither do we know the one necessary course of history, nor do we envisage a definite goal, the one just and enduring order of human affairs.

Since experience is never definitive, I can never learn from experience alone what I should do: "For there is nothing more noxious or more unworthy of a philosopher than the vulgar habit of citing supposedly contrary experience" (i.e., contrary to the Idea). There would be no contrary experience if we promptly followed the Ideas. "It is a perfectly sound Idea, which sets up the maximum as an archetype for men to follow in gradually raising their legal order to the highest attainable perfection. For no one can or should determine the highest stage, where mankind must halt, for freedom can surpass any fixed limit."

Thus Kant demands openness to experience under the absolute guidance of the Idea. The "republican mode of government" presupposes in the people a state of mind which in turn it perpetually engenders: unconditional allegiance to the Idea of right. Analogous to the categorical imperative, right is the ultimate ground of decision; far from deriving its authority from the desire for happiness or from expedience, it sometimes even runs counter to these considerations.

F. This political attitude is concerned only with real possibilities. While advancing toward future experience, the nature of which remains open, it draws ethical motivation from the supersensible. While respecting the uncertainty of the phenomenal world, it is sustained in action by the ethical absolute. While forgoing perfection in time, the magic of an illusory salvation in the world, it is guided by a sense of responsibility which pervades all its thoughts.

Because the final goal cannot be brought about at one stroke and the course of events is slow and gradual, Kant's *ethical* thinking is *revolutionary* (the basis of his new mode of thought is a revolution in the individual, brought about by enlightenment); his political thinking, however, is *evolutionary*.

Kant is a realist in respect to facts and an idealist in regard to the claim of the Idea upon man in his action.

As a realist, he carries skepticism to the extreme, in order to disclose the authentic ground of certainty, which however acts surely and confidently in the medium of reality. Discouragement at facts arouses the courage to change these facts in the course of events.

He is a "pessimist" in regard to the individual man and the particular reality, an "optimist" in regard to the whole.

Kant's historical and political thinking is sustained by his philosophical attitude. It seems intelligible without the philosophy, but then it is reduced to the level of superficial common sense; the underlying power is lost.

6. Objections

A. *Contradictions:* In Kant's political thinking, as in all his philosophy, contradictions can be disclosed. The question is whether they are fundamental to his thinking, or whether they are the only form in which his truth can be expressed.

Contradictions appear when the various planes of Kant's thinking are reduced to a single plane, that of the understanding. In political life, the realms of experience and freedom are so interdependent that contradictions arise whenever the reader substitutes one for the other. The contradictions are an illusion which vanishes when the philosophy is considered as a whole. To seek them out, classify and resolve them, to show the different ways in which they become inevitable requires a thorough analysis, which to some extent has been attempted in our exposition. I myself have concluded that there are very few real contradictions and that these can be corrected.

Kant's thinking never ends in compromise. He does not annul the oppositions and contradictions in favor of a static, flattened middle term. What he conceives as the middle term of his philosophical dualism is an insight that does not flatten out the oppositions but elucidates their origin.

For the Kantian dialectic does not produce rounded, self-contained totalities but opens up new insights. The contradictions are raised to extreme tension. Where they are transcended, it is in the supersensible or in the contemplation of the beautiful or in the infinitely organized tension of living things. In all these cases they are never transcended by knowledge but only by the "reflecting judgment."

B. *Kant's political faith:* Kant awaits and hopes for and in his thinking works actively toward future progress. Although he does not know, he possesses a certainty rooted in practical morality: "Since the human race is steadily advancing in respect to culture, I may be justified in assuming that it is also progressing in respect to the moral purpose of its existence. I take as my foundation my inborn duty to influence those who come after me in such a way that they may become steadily better (accordingly, I must assume that this is possible)." There are possible objections to this faith grounded in practice. An attempt to dispel them may throw light on Kant's meaning.

1. The facts of history—the meaningless ebb and flow of events—argue against Kant's belief in progress. Kant replies: Only if the doubts based on the facts of history "were capable of disproving hope, could they move me to abstain from a seemingly vain endeavor." "As long as this cannot be made wholly certain," I shall not exchange the duty of contributing to progress "for the rule of expedience that tells us not to work for the impossible." "Though I may never know for sure whether better things are to be expected for the human race, this cannot detract from the maxim that hope is possible."

2. Faith is not knowledge; the faith expressed in constructions of the whole consequently makes such knowledge inapplicable to political reality. Kant's answer: In our human situation we can neither theoretically understand nor practically plan the whole course of history. It can only be an idea for us. The thinking that is constitutive of faith is not directed toward any application, but toward certainty. It does not have the utility of available knowledge, but affects my general state of mind, which is the source of my particular thought and action.

We act. But in our planning we can "start only from the parts." The whole "is too big" for us; our Ideas reach out to it but not our influence. Only from Providence can we expect "an outcome that encompasses the whole and thence extends to the parts." That is to say, in our planning and our action, we must leave the course of events open. Accordingly, it is advisable for men "to leave the outcome of their action to Providence." For what the outcome "will be in the course of nature, remains forever uncertain."

3. Kant's assertion that man is progressing not only in regard to cultural goods, political and juridical forms, but also in regard to morality, is contrary to the very nature of morality, which is timeless.

The passages in which Kant speaks of progress in morality should be interpreted in the light of his statement that progress "is not a constantly growing quantity of morality in the conscience, but an increase of the products of its legality through dutiful actions." If there comes to be less violence on the part of the powerful and more compliance with the laws; if men become more reliable in keeping their word; if ultimately all this extends to nations in their dealings with one another and a cosmopolitan society is established—"the moral foundation of the human race will not be increased in the slightest; for that a kind of new Creation (supernatural influence) would be needed." The progress of morality as a whole is to be taken as progress in legality, in the orders and forms of life, in the pathways opened up to the individual by the general improvement. Where the individual is concerned, progress must be forever renewed by a "revolution in thinking."

4. It may be argued that Kant (like the Enlightenment in general) not only indulged in an unfounded optimism in respect to the future but that in absolutizing the future goal he belied his own profound insight into the phenomenality of temporal existence.

This may be said in reply: Kant bases his optimism solely on the practical duty of working for future betterment. Certain facts may argue against the possibility of a realization of reason, but nowhere do we find any proof. In every situation, there remains an "even so," in regard not only to transcendence, but also to the temporal future.

And this too should be considered: Kant does not, like the thinkers of India or like Jesus and the first Christians, consider the possibility that man may become totally corrupt and that the world may face utter destruction. He did not consider perspectives such as those opened up in our time by the hydrogen bomb. But faced with such possibilities, Kant would assuredly maintain his fundamental position. He would continue to demand, without reservation, that though the total result of our action cannot be known, we act in pursuit of the Idea, because such action is the only possible basis for meaningful, rational existence. But perhaps, in envisaging the situation, Kant would distinguish even more sharply between hope for a definite temporal future and the Idea of man which cuts across time. His hope for the future would be limited to the fundamental Idea of a federative world order governed by right, for this he would regard as the only Idea susceptible of guiding mankind toward peace and away from the war that threatens total destruction, the only Idea tending to create an area in which only those human aptitudes which do not imply the destruction of humanity would develop. If this hope should be disappointed, there would remain only the Idea that "cuts across time," disclosed in the cipher of the Kantian postulates. But if our active temporal hope culminates in peace, even this realization derives its value only from the eternal presence of the Idea which in time transcends time. Only a mankind whose existence fulfills it can triumph over destruction and doom. If men do not fulfill this Idea, their existence in itself is without value. "If justice perishes, the life of men on earth loses all value." But to Kant's mind, no man has the right to judge that justice has wholly perished. And even if so terrible a judgment seemed possible, the question would remain: What of the ten, or the two, righteous men in Sodom and Gomorrah? Here again Kant gives no answer.

7. Comparisons

Lessing at one point conceived of history as a process of education in which men's souls attain to purity and perfect reason. History is a total process in which an endless chain of rebirths permits every soul to participate. In contrast to this, Kant conceives of a rightful order based on republics and an association of nations; this rightful order he looks upon as an infinitely remote goal, an Idea leading to a betterment of conditions, not of men's ethical disposition.

According to Hegel, all history is a single movement of the spirit, a now without past or future. For Kant historical development is essential; it brings forth the civil order which makes possible the development of all men's aptitudes, though their intrinsic character remains the same.

Kant's "natural purpose," which from man's purposive action produces something other than what man originally intended, becomes in Hegel the "ruse of the Idea," which employs men and their passions as instruments. His view stems from an unconditional affirmation of actual happening, past and present. Kant does not aspire to knowledge of the total course of history; he wishes, rather, by pointing to a helpful natural purpose whose traces may be discerned by the historical eye, to encourage men to act while taking a sharply critical view of reality.

Hegel composed a magnificent and richly documented universal history. Kant gave no such documented survey He merely set a task: let others, guided by reason, examine the facts of history for traces of a natural purpose. Hegel did not carry out the task set by Kant. Critical verification vanished. And in Hegel the future and the appeal to freedom are also lacking.

Marx seems closer to Kant, but differs in three crucial respects: (1) he reduces everything to an economic dialectic which, he supposes, can be fully known; (2) he abandons historical investigation; that is, instead of considering all the facts of history, even those that contradict his presuppositions, he seeks empirical confirmation of a fundamental hypothesis and neglects other facts; (3) he calls for a single violent upheaval (dictatorship of the proletariat), which is expected, as though by magic, to bring about perfection in human relations in a definite temporal future.

Common to Kant and Marx is the connection between knowledge and will, but Kant's critical limitation of knowledge and hence of the scope of possible planning (exercise of the will) distinguishes him radically from the total knowledge and total planning of Marxist thinking. In Marx, the revolutionary aims at an act of violence, performed by design, anticipated as necessary, and followed by a totalitarian dictatorship; in Kant he aims at a revolution in thinking, which, perpetually renewed in the individual, makes for gradual (evolutionary) progress ad infinitum.

Kierkegaard, who expressed the spiritual crisis of the modern age at the same time as Marx, rejects the philosophy of history as a guide to our action. For it distracts us from the task of being ourselves. Both starting from Hegel, Marx and Kierkegaard take opposite paths. Marx finds the salvation of man in society, Kierkegaard in the individual. Kant's thinking takes in both possibilities. His view of history as a whole and his call for ethical decision are both subjected to critical limitation. As though exploding in different directions, the later thinkers (Kierkegaard, Marx, etc.) lost the fundamental attitude of human reason, which provides a basis for continuity in the building of human reality.

VII. CRITICISM OF KANT

No one has ever taken over the Kantian philosophy without contradicting Kant in essential points. No one can understand him without correcting some of his statements. To understand Kant means to agree with him on fundamentals but to discuss critically many questions closer to the surface. Criticism of this sort rests on the assumption that on the whole Kant took a new way and a true one. The critic has gone through Kant's revolution in thinking for himself; he has become a different man, and now proceeds to ask how, on the ground he has gained with Kant, he is to understand each one of Kant's propositions.

We find, in Kant, three questionable positions which are rooted in the very nature of his thinking and to which he adhered with great firmness. They are questionable because, though there is truth in them, it is not a clear, unequivocal truth. Here in any case there are unsolved difficulties: (1) Kant's philosophy lays claim to the character of a science possessing the same universal validity as mathematics and physics. (2) It claims to provide fundamental a priori insights in regard to the material of the natural sciences and compelling insights in regard to the content of the ethical law (*Metaphysics of Nature* and *Metaphysics of Morals*). This knowledge Kant calls "doctrine" in contradistinction to critique, and he is referring to it when, after concluding his third and last Critique, he writes: "I shall immediately proceed to the doctrinal aspect." (3) Kant's philosophy lays claim to systematic completeness; it is permeated with a multiplicity of systematizations.

Those who criticize Kant on Kantian ground may draw comfort from Kant's own plea to his readers "to understand the author better than he understood himself"; for he was compelled to cast about in search of his ideas and sometimes went astray, while the reader, having the whole work at his disposal, will be in a position to grasp them more easily and with greater certainty. When a critic takes this attitude in contradicting Kant, it is in the intention of modifying formulations on the basis of Kantian thinking. Even where our argument seems to strike at the roots of the Kantian system, we are trying to bring out the positive core of statements in which perhaps Kant has not been faithful to his own thinking.

1. *The Scientific Character of Kant's Philosophy*

Kant claimed that with him philosophy for the first time had entered upon the "sure path of a science." He compared his new method with the leap which had once led from multiple experience to mathematics as a science, from heterogeneous observation to modern science. It was this initial leap that made possible steady scientific progress in contrast to the previous vicissitudes of beclouded opinion. In this sense, Kant was convinced that he had supplied a "totally new science." He compares his method (in solving the antinomies of metaphysics through his insight into the phenomenal character of things in space and time) with the experimental method of the scientists. For Kant the solution of contradictions is science. "Only that science whose certainty is apodictic can be called true science." And he claimed such certainty for his philosophy. This he often repeated: "Metaphysics must be a science, or else it is nothing at all." Here conjectures are worthless. His new "metaphysic of metaphysics" would be in vain if it wished only to "mitigate its failures by deploring the limits of our reason and reducing its assertions to mere conjectures." "For unless the impossibility of such conjectures is demonstrated and unless the self-knowledge of reason has become a true science by which the field where it is futile and fruitless to apply reason is marked off as it were with geometrical certainty, all those idle endeavors will never cease." But in a positive sense this science is the elucidation of the entire use of reason.

My interpretation of Kant is based "on the letter" and on the organization of the whole. In this method, we no longer classify Kant's statements as true and false, but try to interpret them according to their meaning in the whole. We interpret positively, pointing out the meaning of each proposition (not negatively, i.e., excluding many of Kant's statements in favor of some particular line of thought which is singled out from the whole).

This principle of interpretation is a stumbling block for those who aspire to definite, objective knowledge in philosophy as in the sciences. It seems to contradict Kant's own demand for apodictic certainty. By taking into account everything that Kant said, we appear to contradict him in this fundamental position. But perhaps this seemingly justified impression will be dispelled if we show the very particular way in which Kant defined his philosophy as a science.

According to Kant, his philosophy is a science by virtue of its "method and system." It "cannot be gathered piece by piece; rather, its germ must be completely preformed in critique." Such is the special character of this science "that it can be established at one stroke in its complete and permanent state, that it can neither be advanced in the least, nor amplified nor modified, by any subsequent discovery."

Kant identified his painstaking progress from step to step with scientific method. The systematic labor of testing, rejecting, and new testing was required not by the original idea, which was already present and complete, but by the necessity of translating it into clear thought. For he could not content himself with the aphoristic formulation of a profound insight; he demanded the clarity of a whole system which, once finished, would communicate a full consciousness of being to those who would re-enact its operations. A work of this sort required long effort, for everything had to be considered in relation to everything else; and understanding on the part of the reader also demanded long effort. The fact that the whole idea was formed in his mind from the very start misled Kant for years into supposing that his work would be quickly concluded. And the strict organization that proved indispensable to the unfolding of his system under the guidance of an Idea misled him into supposing that he was carrying on the scientific investigation of an object.

Kant still lived in the age-old tradition in which thinking was regarded as a science, provided only that a systematic method was observed. The vast intellectual effort of philosophy was looked upon as "science," that is, as rational activity. It had always claimed universal validity for all, presenting itself as the one truth. But it was Kant (and not Descartes, as is often supposed) who first created an awareness of the imperious currents which have since then led to the basic self-awareness of modern science and in so doing revolutionized the methods of philosophy. Kant's philosophy stood at the dividing line between two worlds. Living in the old philosophical world, he laid the foundations of the new one.

If we propound such alternatives as science or edifying discourse, compelling science or irresponsible opinion, Kant's thinking has no place on one side or the other, or even in between.

Philosophizing with the transcendental method is not a science like other sciences, because it has no object and because the method itself cannot be clearly defined. But it is comparable to science not only because it claims to provide compelling insights, but also because its insights, once understood, are actually experienced as "scientifically compelling" in a sense which perhaps can be defined.

We have tried to define it in discussing Kant's "theory of knowledge." Since there is no object to be grasped, the understanding incurs a "compelling" failure, which is reflected in the intricate texture of methods of approach and modes of representation (psychological, logical, methodological, metaphysical; the forms of tautology, vicious circle, and contradiction; the phenomenological, constructive, argumentative methods) all pointing to the truth of the original thought. Thereby the reader who participates in Kant's thinking is "compellingly" delivered from the prison of the phenomenality of existence. Of course this delivery cannot be compellingly known as we know a thing, but it can be compellingly experienced as an intellectual illumination which forms the basis of my new consciousness of being. But the "whither" of my delivery is compelling in neither of the two senses. In every case, reason must draw the material of its fulfillment from outside itself: in the sciences, from systematic observation or intuitive construction; in ethical practice and the contemplation of the beautiful, from the supersensible.

The Kantian method of transcending resembles compelling science in another respect: it operates without personal engagement, unhistorically, as a pure function of the self-understanding of reason. Its universal thought processes, in which reason speaks to reason in pure form without particular content, provide the possibility of a reciprocal, impersonal, unhistorical understanding among men as rational beings, each in his finite existential situation. In its method, this universal thinking is very close to objective scientific thought. But the communication we find in it has greater depth and scope than any communication based on scientific knowledge.

Yet in spite of all this, there can be no doubt that Kant's transcendental philosophy cannot be termed scientific if by science we mean what modern science aims at and achieves: the systematic, universally valid, compelling knowledge of particular objects. A purely circumstantial objection to Kant's claim is that his insight is far from having gained the universal acceptance that would have been accorded a truly scientific insight.

2. The Way to the Doctrine

The scientific character of Kantian philosophy discloses a new ambiguity when we consider the transition from "critique" to "doctrine."

A. *Propaedeutic and doctrine:* Kant calls his critique a "treatise on method," not a system of science itself. It is a "propaedeutic" for a "future system of metaphysics." Accordingly, he distinguishes "critique" from "doctrine" and writes in the preface to the third Critique (the *Critique of Judgment*): "Here then I end my whole critical undertaking. I shall proceed without delay to the doctrine." The doctrine will be concerned with two fields, the "Metaphysics of Nature" and the "Metaphysics of Morals."

What is doctrine? In the Kantian sense, it is the elaboration of concrete and definite a priori knowledge of nature and morality. Kant says we shall gain "an a priori knowledge, hence a metaphysics," of the objects that are given to us a posteriori, "if from experience we take nothing more than is needed to give us an object," in our external sense the concept of matter, in our inner sense the empirical representation of a thinking being. But actually this step to doctrine is only the last in the development that began when Kant derived the categories and principles from their source in the "I think" (transcendental apperception). These a priori forms are of many kinds (each of which is stressed in its place): the "faculties of the mind" (thought, will, feeling), the forms of intuition (space and time), the table of judgments and categories, the three Ideas, the schematisms of time, the system of principles, the concepts of reflection.

Principles which, according to Kant, have a priori validity for all knowledge of nature are, for example: All intuitions are extensive magnitudes. In all phenomena, the reality which is an object of sensation has intensive magnitude, that is, a degree. Amid all the changes of phenomena, the substance remains unchanged. All changes occur in accordance with the law of cause and effect.

B. *The doctrinal endeavor was in vain:* In his old age, Kant went to the greatest pains to formulate his "doctrine." Even after completing the *Metaphysics of Nature,* he kept looking for a "bridge" from this metaphysics of nature to physics, as a number of his posthumous notations bear witness. But compared to the critical works, the whole undertaking aroused little interest. Even in the critical works, the complete set of categories and principles has never captured much attention. Each reader singles out particular ones (such as the principles of substance and causality), forgetting the rest of the list.

Kant's doctrinal metaphysics has not been recognized by the natural sciences. On the philosophical side, it has little importance for an understanding of Kant's philosophy of reason. In both these respects, Kant's doctrinal endeavors were in vain. This state of affairs can only be clarified by criticism of Kant which, if properly carried out, will at the same time safeguard the substance of the philosophy against modern attempts to destroy the whole edifice by disclosing particular errors.

C. *A priori forms not possible without a posteriori factors and vice versa:* In taking the step from a priori to a posteriori, Kant employs a "middle link." In the transition from the categories to the experience to which they apply (or from the pure forms to sensory experience) the middle link is the "schema of the imagination," which is subject to the intuitive forms of time; the last middle link is the representation of the datum as matter.

The a priori forms are not possible without a posteriori factors. Kant acknowledges as much by saying that here our derivation comes up against a limit and that it remains a mystery why we encounter just these forms and this number of forms. The fundamental situation may be stated as follows: in all particular, determinate knowledge there is an a priori factor; but conversely, beginning with the very first derivation (from the one a priori origin) every a priori form contains an a posteriori factor.

D. *How the doctrinal endeavor may be criticized:* Kant was aware that the transcendental deduction of the particular from the universal was open to question. He tries to remedy the difficulty by distinguishing transcendental thinking, which, in the knowledge of the conditions of objectivity, anticipates essential features of the objective content, from mere logical thinking, which cannot derive the particular from the universal, but can only subsume the given under the universal. Kant says that transcendental thinking is distinguished not only "by its rank in respect to universality," but also "by a very special mode."

Mere universality would not clearly distinguish the a priori from the empirical. Where, in a descending series of this kind ("since we do not distinguish that which is wholly a priori from that which is only known a posteriori") "shall we draw the line that would divide the uppermost links from the last? . . . Does the concept of extension pertain to metaphysics . . . or that of the body? . . . or of the fluid body? . . . if we continue in this manner, everything will become a part of metaphysics." Thus a limit cannot be determined by the degree of the particular's subordination to the universal, but only by "total dissimilarity and diversity of origin."

From this totally diverse origin, Kant believes he can develop a doctrine of "metaphysics" in which the question of where the dividing line is to be drawn between a priori and a posteriori vanishes. It is striking to note that in trying to erect a doctrinal metaphysics on a critical foundation Kant, quite as a matter of course, reintroduces the old names of the philosophical disciplines: thus, he terms the part dealing with the development of concepts, "which refer to objects as such without presupposing any given objects," "ontology" (which he had spurned as a proud and presumptuous name); while he subsumes the concepts relating to nature as the aggregate of given objects under the title of "rational physiology," etc.

But objectively we may say this: If Kant looks upon the "I think" of transcendental apperception as the condition of the possibility of all objects, it means that for him the a priori is, in all knowledge, distinct from the a posteriori. But when he goes on to derive from the "I think," first the categories, then the principles of knowledge of nature, two fundamentally different trains of thought become intertwined: first, the elucidation (in the Transcendental Deduction) of the phenomenon of objectivity through the objective representations which serve as guiding threads and the operations which serve as means of clarification; and second, the supposedly unequivocal and universally valid derivation of definite principles governing our knowledge of nature.

The transcendental method as an elucidation of the fundamental situation of consciousness as such and of its modes of objectivity carries philosophical conviction. But convincing as it may be, the thesis that all objectivity is conditioned by subjective forms of the "I think" provides no foundation for the definite derivation and complete systematization of the modes of experience. Kant himself says: We discern the a priori forms not in experience, but on the occasion of experience. From this we may infer, as Kant did not, that future experience may provide the occasion on which new a priori forms will become known. Where the occasion of experience has not yet occurred, the a priori can in fact not yet be known.

When a derivation is attempted after experience, the a posteriori factor which fills the forms is always present. Kant took Newtonian physics as his guide. Today we have a far more comprehensive physics, in which Newton's is only an element.

Conversely, in rising to the first categories and principles, we never attain to the absolutely "pure" a priori. Just as there is an a priori in every empirical concept, so, in the first category of the "I think," there is also an a posteriori. The first steps from the "I think" to the concrete and particular are not known solely through the self-elucidation of reason, but are occasioned by experience and then elaborated as pure a priori forms.

Thus even though the fundamental insight of the Kantian philosophy is fully convincing, its doctrinal derivations are subject to correction and refutation. But this does not detract from the fundamental insight.

One might have supposed that Kant, who insisted so strongly on the role of experience, who recognized that no cognition can have objective validity without intuition and attached so much importance to what we cannot produce but which is given to us from without—one might have supposed that he would limit philosophy to critique and leave all doctrine to the decision of the empirical sciences.

This was not the case. Particularly in his later years, he cast a blemish on his philosophy by building an extensive doctrine on a prior construction. Critique, as he understood it, could supply definite knowledge in regard to nature and morality. Thus critique became something more than a means of elucidating our consciousness of the phenomenality of existence and examining the limits and origins of what is being for us; taking on the function of objective knowledge, it became a source of empirical judgments that no experience can confute, because they are the ground of experience. Thus

the universal laws which we—the subject as such—impose on nature become philosophical doctrine, while the special laws, which can only be discovered by experience, are the field of the empirical sciences. But the truth
is that all theoretical laws are experiments along the endless path of scientific
investigation, and it is only through experience that they acquire validity.
According to Kant's doctrine, there would have been no point in the geodetic
investigations by which Gauss proved to his own satisfaction that the three
angles of a triangle actually added up to two right angles, or in the painstaking experiments by which nineteenth-century chemists sought to determine whether the quantity of substance in a body was invariable or not.
When at first all these experiments merely seemed to confirm the soundness of Kant's principles, these gained in prestige. And yet the un-Kantian
methods turned out to be meaningful. For today the laws then thought
to be absolute are no longer looked upon as such. Within definable spheres
of experience they are valid; but in the realms of the very small and the
very large, they have given way to other laws. Kant's critical philosophy has
sustained its encompassing truth in opposition to his own doctrinal constructions. His philosophy is still right over against the absolutizations of any
definite natural insights, whether stemming from scientists or fixated by Kant
himself in his "doctrine."

E. *Examples of the true meaning of Kant's statements about nature:* Perhaps
we can make our meaning somewhat clearer. Unlike Kant's constructions of matter and force, his philosophical thinking in regard to the antinomies and the world as Idea is still perfectly tenable. In rejecting such
propositions as "The world is finite," "The world is infinite," and saying
instead: Let us inquire endlessly in the world; the world as a whole is not
an object but an Idea—he is still right. Even though Einstein may have
calculated that the cosmos is finite, even though it has been computed that
the world began five billion years ago, every thinking being must still
grant the validity of Kant's demand: Continue to investigate, try to go still
further.

If the notion of progress ad infinitum has to be abandoned for Euclidean
space, we can seek our "ad infinitum" in a different direction—e.g., the
current conception of an expanding universe. If a finite beginning is posited,
we can still ask: What went before, or what were the presuppositions or
conditions of the beginning? (Or we can dismiss the question, saying:
Before the beginning there was no time, there was nothing. But that is to
change the whole basis of our thinking in favor of a Creation metaphysics
on the Augustinian style.) Or if space is infinite, we can still inquire into
new dimensions; and beyond causality and statistics, we can still search for
broader, more comprehensive relations. But, again in line with Kant, no
speculations, either metaphysical or mathematical, are valid for our knowledge of the world. Speculative constructions are significant only insofar as

they guide us in our observation and so increase our experience. They have no scientific value in themselves and can never lead to a knowledge of the world as a whole (and this applies even to the "cosmic formula" developed mathematically by Einstein toward the end of his life—a construction that can lead to no observation and cannot be verified).

F. *Summary*

1. Kant himself does not represent the critique as a universal elucidation of reason; he does not explicitly say that its purpose, a philosophical transformation of consciousness, is something radically different from doctrine. But in his remarks on philosophy we find significant utterances in this direction.

2. The doctrine goes back to the very beginnings of the critique. The critique goes deepest where it is least concerned with the classifications that are the beginning of the doctrine.

3. Every aspect of the critique with which Kant elucidates our consciousness of being suggests ideas of the utmost relevance for our approach to the sciences. Even if nothing in the critique anticipated the doctrine, it would throw invaluable light on the nature and limits of science and on the principles that govern its thinking.

4. In the "Transcendental Deduction" there is no mention of definite categories; dealing with the possibility of objects and of all experience, it presents Kant's critical thinking in its widest scope. After that his perspective narrows: from objective knowledge as such to scientific objectivity and then, still further, to mathematical science.

The operation carried out in the "Transcendental Deduction" is far more comprehensive—in respect both to possible a priori forms and to possible intuition—than what remains after objectivity has been narrowed down to Newtonian physics as mathematical science. In studying Kant, we must start by following him along the thread that he took as his guide, but in so doing we must win for ourselves the realm opened up by his essential critical insights.

G. *Comparison with Hegel:* Though the differences between them are fundamental, Kant and Hegel have one thing in common: an uncritical attitude. Hegel has it from the start and throughout his philosophizing (for him critique and doctrine are one); with Kant (who tried to distinguish between critique and doctrine), it begins only where he embarks on doctrine. In Hegel's philosophy, one might say, an initial critique of being unfolds by absorbing the matter of the world. Kant's philosophy does not remain within the bounds of critique but is oriented toward a construction of reality that spreads to every sphere of existence. Beginning with the *Metaphysics of Nature* and the *Metaphysics of Morals,* his purpose, of defining the scope, the limits, and the direction of scientific inquiry, is enlarged and falsified by an intervention of doctrine. But in Hegel the doctrine, his positive

theory of a total world process, is dominant, while in Kant the critique remains the effective philosophical force, beside which the doctrine never takes on essential importance.

3. The System

The scientific character of the philosophy is further diminished when we consider its claim to be a "system."

Kant speaks of the "structure" of the whole and asks the reader to bear it in mind when considering the particular: "Pure reason is a sphere so closely articulated that one can touch no part of it without coming into contact with all the rest." From the very outset Kant's purpose was to produce a complete system: it must be possible to "survey" the field of reason, "because it lies a priori in ourselves" (November 24, 1776).

Viewing Kant's work as a whole, we must now ask: Was he successful in expressing his view of totality? Did he build a fully articulated system? The answer must be: He worked out and formulated systematizations, but he did not derive them from one principle and weave them together. We can distinguish layers of systematization: the divisions of his works do not coincide with the underlying system (for example, the dichotomic divisions of the *Critique of Pure Reason:* doctrine of elements—doctrine of method; aesthetics—logic; analytic—dialectic, do not coincide with the essential structure of knowledge, the trichotomy: forms of intuition, categories, Ideas). We can juxtapose the various elements of classification and show how they are used. Following the last *Critique,* we can give preference to a schema that was essential to Kant: nature, freedom, and the mediating "faculty of reflecting judgment" (in the contemplation of the beautiful and in biological knowledge). We note Kant's systematizations and the arrangements that serve merely as methods of exposition. We note his evident delight in any sort of order and above all his passion for systematic completeness. But we never find "the system." That is a fact to which none of the particular systematizations should blind us. And it seems to me that unless we recognize this fact, the depth of Kant's thinking must be lost to us. But Kant himself did not recognize it. It is of the greatest interest to investigate Kant's striving to set up a system, and follow it through all his systematizations.

In none of its particular forms does Kant's system give his entire thought. Yet the Idea of system, around which Kant seems to circle, remains valid. Like all Kant's Ideas, it is not given but imposed as an endless task! But here—in the system of reason—Kant aspires to complete it and believes he has done so. The conviction of having grasped the truth of the Idea irrevocably and forever, is transformed into the belief that the particular system he has set up in his investigation of reason is complete and definitive. But even in the transcendental elucidation of reason as a whole, the Idea, in every one of its forms, leads only to a provisional schema. It hovers, it circles, it guides us aloft and into the depths. But it cannot be fixated in any perfect form. We should say: The Idea is forever true; that is essentially a matter of conviction—but the embodiment of the Idea is subject to discussion. Meaningful discussion is possible only where there is common belief in the Idea. Where such conviction is present (though it cannot be adequately defined) the particular embodiments of the Idea are open to boundless transformation.

None of Kant's explicit systematizations captures reason as a whole. They are provisional crystallizations—the thought bursts their bounds and then they are in need of revision. They are schemata which can lead to new perspectives and discoveries. In any attempt to set forth the Kantian system, we are reduced to one of these many systematizations, and essential ideas are lost because they do not fit into the "system" we have selected. The many systematizations do not add up to a system.

Kant's idealist disciples regarded this as a great weakness and were determined to correct it by deriving an all-encompassing system from a single principle. To my mind, it is the superior merit of Kant that his integrity led him to do what the nature of his investigations demanded. But Kant himself, as his work grew, did not retain his clarity in this point. He did not yet know the adversary whose path he himself had opened. In his old age, he confused the final validity of his fundamental attitude toward reason with the supposed validity of the conceptual form of his philosophy. Already on the brink of senile dementia, he had barely the strength to rebuff the great adversary he sensed among his youthful devotees with the words: "God save us from our friends; we ourselves will be on guard against our enemies." But Kant was no longer able to express the truth of his cause in a polemic capable of withstanding the magic spell of these brilliant young men.

4. *The Limits of Kant's Philosophy*

Kant's philosophy communicates no vision of the world. It creates no symbols. It is a sober philosophy, and its very sobriety brings out the unique power of the form—to awaken sources, to open paths, to activate the ultimate standards, to *enable*.

This philosophy never verges on poetry (unless we count the explicit metaphors which never claim to be ideas); it is critique; that is, it differentiates and sets limits and, in so doing, clears the way; it confirms and justifies insights that were already present, clarifies our consciousness of them, and encourages us in following them out.

Consequently, it is not self-sufficient. (It does not, like certain philosophies, Schopenhauer's for instance, present itself as something akin to a poem.)

The limits set by this philosophy are inherent in its thinking. They are the limits of the forms. Kant forgoes richness of content, because he wishes

to convey a pure consciousness of the "forms." Forms are superior to philosophical embodiment, because, if I think them through, they make me produce my thinking. They act upon my nonobjective inwardness, my freedom.
Forms have the power to awaken. They give shape to my thinking and
must therefore be complemented by reality: by individual *Existenz,* scientific
inquiry, historical vision, the contemplation of art and poetry. Along our
historical pathways, the philosophical thoughts born of faith in reason are
orientations, lines of exploration, means of critical verification; they are not
concrete programs.

There is greatness in Kant's thinking of limits and forms. This means that
the formal power of Kant's philosophy resides in Kant's own thinking, not
in any academic knowledge of Kantian concepts. Kantian scholasticism is
more threadbare than any other.

To grasp the greatness of Kant's thinking presupposes a basic existential
decision. Kant leaves many men dissatisfied, as though deprived of food and
air. They yearn for a transcendent content and are unprepared to live by
Kantian reason with the imageless God.

The criticism implied in this attitude may contain a grain of truth, though
the critics themselves misunderstand it because they lose sight of Kant's
thinking. Let us look into this truth.

Limits that define a field and thus create a new space can become restrictive
if the field does not remain open. The unique power of definition, or rational
form, may, when the philosophy is elaborated in the work, destroy the philosophy's power to transcend rational form. Between the imageless God, the
range of worldly experience, and the contemplation of the beautiful there exists a world in which symbols speak to us, or rather where the particular becomes a symbol of the universal. This is the world of each man's struggle for
the historical meaning of his own *Existenz.* There are possibilities of elucidating *Existenz* which, without negating or even restricting reason, go beyond it.
This brings us to something which is not to be found in Kant, and which,
where it appears in another philosophy, does not refute Kant but complements him and complements his purifying reason.

A. *History:* Kant's historical consciousness is not explicit. He seems to be
concerned solely with the timeless, the law of nature, the law of freedom,
the genius that produces the timeless in works of art, the supersensible
substrate of humanity.

But the laws of nature and freedom relate to the temporal phenomenon.
Works of poetry and art do not result merely from genius as a natural gift,
which by its very essence would be the same at all times. *This* nature has its
source in a man who lives in his own historical time and understands himself through the play of images he creates; it springs from the historicity of
mankind and of each man, who is always an individual.

The awareness that something eternal is decided in time, the paradox of the historical consciousness of *Existenz,* is discernible in Kant, but it is not expressed in statements that give this consciousness a self-consciousness.

Kant read history and travel books and took an interest in historical reality. But in his works on the philosophy of history, in his *Anthropology,* he turns back to the timeless: he is concerned with the total course of history and in it more with the future than the past; amid the many appearances, he is concerned with the enduring essence of man.

He had no intimation of the vast development of historical knowledge and ideas, oriented exclusively toward the past, that would set in with Hegel and the "Historical School." Kierkegaard and Nietzsche reacted to this "historicism" insofar as it had degenerated into a mere collecting of facts or the aesthetic contemplation of the past as a kind of panorama or picture book. Kant would have supported them in their struggle for the seriousness of *Existenz* against the aimlessly eclectic contemplation of the past. Yet the historical sciences brought to light a captivating reality which, seen in conjunction with the historical *Existenz* of the individual, has raised questions which, existentially as well as historically, are still very much alive. All this was beyond Kant's horizon.

B. *The "I think"*: The riddle of the "I think" (that thinking I am) is at the very center of Kant's philosophizing, but no solution is arrived at. Kant's "I think," that "must be able to accompany all our representations," is still far from the "I am" of the existential consciousness (it is only consciousness as such); nor is it the empirical "I am" in the manifold of its appearances.

Even though the ethically acting, free personality led Kant to the intelligible character, this ethical character was only the impersonal, universal being of the rational good will. In Kant's written work (not in the substance of his thinking) we find only the old distinction between the universal and the particular (in intuition); what is lacking is the distinction between the universal and the historical personality (of law and of *Existenz*). Thus the Kantian universal has a pathos which it derives only from its identification (occasionally expressed) with the personal. The "I think" is the most abstract and at the same time most essential motif in Kant's critique of reason. What it leaves open is capable of closing in the rationalistic distortions of Kantian thinking.

C. *Love:* Kant seldom speaks of love and when he does, what he says is inadequate. He seems to explore and elucidate the whole realm of reason without perceiving that in a sense reason is love and operates in love. This remained outside his philosophical scope.

D. *Pessimism:* Kant was capable of judgments on life as a whole, which conflict with nearly all his philosophizing. This may be noted in his treatise on *The Failure of All Philosophical Attempts at a Theodicy* (1791), in which he sets out to show that certain questions are beyond reason and that any attempt to solve them by reason can only lead to pseudo knowledge and futile opinions. It contains judgments that are not motivated by reason but merely disclose a profound dissatisfaction with life.

In speaking of theodicies, Kant says that reason is absolutely incapable of understanding the connection between the supreme wisdom and a world which experience shows us to be intolerable.

1. Some say that it is wrong to suppose that evil is preponderant, because every man, however wretched his circumstances, would rather be alive than dead. We can refute this "sophistry," says Kant, by asking any man of sound understanding, who has lived long enough and reflected on the value of life, whether he would like to start the game of life all over again. His answer would be no.

2. Some try to justify God by saying that the preponderance of pain over pleasure is inseparable from the animal nature of man. Kant replies: Why did the author of our existence give us life in the first place if it is not desirable for us?

3. Some say that the immeasurable beatitude of the hereafter must be preceded by an earthly life of toil and tribulation, in which we should battle every obstacle to become worthy of the glory to come. To this Kant says: It is absolutely impossible to understand why this period of trial, to which most men succumb and from which even the best of us derive little enjoyment, should be the indispensable condition of the joys to come. To speak of God's supreme wisdom is not to untie the knot but to cut through it.

Kant does not for a moment think of questioning God or the moral law, for they are grounded not in theoretical but in practical reason. But in justly condemning the theodicies, he at the same time condemns man's affirmation of life, in judgments which are not necessitated by reason and which take no account of the power of love.

E. *Ambiguities:* For Kant time is the formal framework of our entire consciousness of the world and of our empirical self-consciousness. From this it follows that our existence is phenomenal, while our true being, our freedom, cuts across time. But in his elaboration of this idea, immortality appears as a postulate to compensate for the imperfection of existence. This leads to ambiguities. He says on the one hand that though our practical reason, grounded in ethical action, is certain of immortality, we can form no representation of it. But, on the other hand, immortality is conceived as occurring in the future and thus becomes a representation. It would no doubt have been impossible for Kant to make it clear in every one of his statements that there is a distinction between a rational postulate and a symbol or methodological formula by which thought is consciously raised above time, so that everything we call past and future becomes a symbol for something else that is timeless. Yet this is the substance of his thought.

On the one hand, he speaks of the progress, not of morality but of legality. But, on the other hand, the Idea governing our duty in political action does not at all times remain only Idea; something calls to us from the real temporal future. On the one hand, Kant speaks of the "end of all things," once again a notion that cuts across time. But, on the other hand, his conceptions of the real end in time and of the timeless end of all time flow together. Kant's morality grounded in the good will is a truth that will never be lost. The critical question is: Is there not something lacking in this truth, namely, the love which, far from being mere "inclination," is also "immortality" and reason and the force which animates all reason?

These last limitations of Kant's philosophizing are not inherent in the thinking itself, but in the necessarily limited personality of the thinker. Those who participate in Kant's thinking must complement it in such a way as to unfold its full truth and power.

5. Kant's Cast of Mind

Kant strove to act in the world as the only place accessible to man. He did not regard himself as a wise man or as a saint situated outside it. If he labored to create a better school of philosophy, it was in the interest of worldly wisdom. He had no wish to stand apart; what he sought in philosophy was something which helps the human race, which helps each man as a man, to do his task.

Thought is of no value without communicability. Kant strove for understanding, communication, peace, but in the movement of life. His goal was not the contentment of an animal at pasture, the tranquillity that corrupts, but the all-embracing reason which links all man's potentialities together and permits them to unfold. No other thinker of the Enlightenment attained to so lofty a concept of reason.

Kant was open to the world, even to its remotest aspects. He respected intelligence and human stature wherever he found them: "Because philosophy can use everything that the man of letters or the eccentric visionary provides, a philosopher values everything that demonstrates a certain strength of mind. Moreover, he is accustomed to taking different standpoints and, because he never loses sight of the mysterious character of the whole, he distrusts his own judgment. . . . Philosophy makes a man humble, or rather, it teaches him to measure himself by the Idea and not in comparison to others." Kant's sense of humanity raised him above all philosophical arrogance, although the lucidity and range of his thinking made him dangerously superior to all his contemporaries.

6. On the Interpretation of Kant

An understanding of Kant cannot be prescribed. Everyone who wishes to philosophize, at once on his own original ground and within the historic tradition, must open-mindedly immerse himself in Kant to see what ideas come to him in the process. There are directives that he will do well to follow.

It is necessary to study works *about* Kant. But they provide only a basis for understanding, not the understanding itself. As we have seen, no one has produced a successful exposition of Kant's philosophical edifice. Thus the second and essential step is to find out what Kant actually did in his thinking, to examine the methods of which Kant himself was perhaps not fully aware, and to penetrate Kant's fundamental philosophical attitude, which found its expression in the work as a whole.

Criticism of Kant presupposes interpretation in three stages:

1. In regard to statements of fact, a critic is perfectly right in pointing out errors, for Kant, like every other thinker, was limited by the scientific development of his time. Certain of Kant's statements on science must be rejected or corrected, but this has little bearing on the thought as a whole.

2. It is necessary to point out logical contradictions. But then the question arises: May a discrepancy not have a special necessity within this logic of transcending and thus prove in the end to be no discrepancy at all?

3. In regard to the standpoint of the whole, we must ask: What is a "standpoint" in philosophy? Clearly it is not permissible to characterize and at the same time dismiss a philosophy by subsuming it under a total concept, for a philosophical standpoint is not definable, it cannot be stated in simple unequivocal terms. Such an operation would be possible only if there were another standpoint from which the standpoint in question could be clearly viewed. And this "outside" standpoint would have to be one that is not itself characterized by a rational and formulable position and that is not a rational premise such as we take as a basis for limited scientific investigations. But the outside standpoint would not be definable. Thus it is in the nature of philosophical "standpoints" (how inappropriate a word!) that we stand in them and cannot survey or order them from outside. In attempting to understand them, we are embarking on an endless task.

VIII. KANT'S HISTORICAL POSITION,
INFLUENCE, AND SIGNIFICANCE FOR OUR TIME

1. *Enlightenment*

Enlightenment is the Western movement in which men, prompted by belief in reason, strove for a natural knowledge of the world, ethics, the state, religion. Characterized by an affirmation of existence, enthusiasm for progress and the perspectives of the future, it is sustained by the will to freedom in thought and politics. It undertakes the venture of human independence; motivated by the Idea of humanity, it makes man a purpose in himself.

It is not enough to say that Kant was the summit and culmination of the Enlightenment. Plato may be called the summit of the Sophist enlightenment in the sense that he mastered it and went beyond it. In the same sense Kant surpassed the eighteenth-century Enlightenment to discover the never-concluded process by which man, through an inner revolution, comes truly to himself.

The Enlightenment was a universal Western movement. It brought scientific positivism, constructive metaphysics on the rational-dogmatic foundation laid by Leibniz, the political liberalism of Locke and Montesquieu, the cultivated emotional life of the Platonists and Romantics. Kant did not negate these tendencies, but limited them and went beyond them. His thinking did not achieve general acceptance in the West, or even in Germany. A good many philosophical movements, nearly all of them in Germany, started from Kant, or took their orientation in opposition to him. Some of the problems he had raised were discussed on every hand. However, the general appraisal of Kant oscillated between extreme admiration and utter rejection.

The substance of the Enlightenment, as reflected in its foremost representatives, is not Kantian thinking; the Enlightenment was the foundation of Kant's thinking but does not encompass it. Rather, it was Kant who, by opening new horizons, limited, defined, and justified the attitudes and achievements of the Enlightenment.

2. German Idealism

It is important to note that Kant defined his philosophical method only incidentally (e.g., in his apt distinction between mathematical and philosophical knowledge). Knowledge of the method is essential to an understanding of Kant. He knew that he was building a "metaphysic of metaphysics," but remained magnificently unaware of the forms and methods of his thinking.

That is why the young enthusiasts and philosophical conquerors of the next generation were able to take him as their starting point. They did not suspect the discipline of his method. They transformed and distorted the clear operations of transcendental thinking into speculative constructions, intellectual visions in which they tell us what God was thinking before and during the Creation. They were responsible for the disastrous transformation of reason into spirit and the confusion between reason and spirit. They ignored the limits set by Kant. In their thinking, which had begun with Kant, Kantian reason was submerged. From the very start they abandoned his basic philosophical attitude. It is in this sense that German Idealism began with Kant. Hegel drew up a schema of philosophical development:

Kant, Fichte, Schelling, Hegel; and to this day it is accepted by most historians of philosophy.

Actually, these thinkers tacitly dropped or expressly rejected Kant's decisive positions from the first. Multidimensional reason was replaced by derivation from a principle; awareness of the finite, discursive character of human reason gave way to a supposed intuitive understanding. Elucidation of reason as the place where being is manifested was set aside in favor of an immediate knowledge of being. Casting off Kant's humility, these philosophers thought the thoughts of God.

By the time Kant died in 1804, many young men had forgotten him. Their minds had been captivated by the magic of the young geniuses. The magic began with untruth—the uncritical neglect of all limits—and in untruth it continued. This common trait of those who had fallen away from Kant admitted of fascinating, mutually antagonistic works: the penetrating constructions of Fichte, the gnostic visions of Schelling, Hegel's magnificent vision of all being in a system of dialectical operations.

3. *Neo-Kantianism*

And then, almost overnight, the magic lost its power. This was the so-called collapse of German Idealism. Now a new Kantianism came into being. The positive sciences—natural and historical—had triumphed. The prestige of philosophy had declined. The uncritical magic was followed by an equally uncritical but shallow and chaotic materialism. From what remained of the philosophical spirit, the cry arose: Back to Kant. Scientists (Helmholtz) believed that in Kant they had found a philosophical justification of their empiricism. Academic philosophers in their eagerness to play a role (other than the teaching of philosophy) in this age of scientific superstition discovered a philosophy of science in Kant's "theory of knowledge." Philosophy became the handmaiden of science.

At the beginning of the twentieth century, a dissatisfaction with this "Neo-Kantianism" made itself felt, but the outlook of the academic pseudo philosophers remained unchanged. The consequence was not a deeper penetration of Kant's philosophy but a kind of repetition of post-Kantian philosophy. Attempts were made to do something new with Fries, Fichte, Schelling, Hegel. For a moment it appeared as though Hegel as the culmination of the process would revive in all his glory. But all these efforts without exception were lacking in philosophical originality; their proponents were never anything more than epigones of epigones. Still no one recognized the gulf between Kant and the Idealists (with the sole exception of Ebbinghaus, who early in the century announced a new interpretation of all of Kant but unfortunately never finished his book).

4. *The Present*

The whole Neo-Kantian movement can be summed up in two catchwords: "Back to Kant" (Liebmann) and "to understand Kant means to go beyond Kant" (Windelband). Both were misused. "To go back" meant to find fixed, eternal truths in Kant, to sift them out from the dross and reinstate them. "To go beyond" meant to do better than Kant, to gain deeper insight. A better interpretation would have made it possible to combine the two ideas. "To go back" would mean to look for the source; and "to go beyond" would mean, not to know better, but to enter into the movement of Kant's creative thinking, to let it act within one's own self in the new situation.

Kant is a nodal point in modern philosophy. His work contains as many possibilities as life itself. Consciously, Kant proceeded with rational precision, yet his work is shot through with thoughts that go beyond the "system" and that Kant in turn strove to understand as part of his doctrine. It remains a source of boundless inspiration.

So far Kant's direct influence has resulted in two main currents: Idealism and Neo-Kantianism. Today, we can see that they were both misunderstandings. Kant himself stands unchanged, superior to his interpreters. Now, for the third time, the fate of philosophy hinges on our attitude toward Kant. It is not possible to know objectively, once and for all, what Kant was and what he thought. He was a creative thinker, who remains more than what he created. He has not been incorporated into something larger; he has not been surpassed, or reduced to one possibility among others. Kant's work is unique in the history of philosophy. Since Plato no one has created such a revolution in Western thought.

At the risk that the reader may not immediately succeed in following in all points, I have tried to explain what Kant's thinking is about. The account of Kant is the most difficult in this book. To possess yourself of Kant (so far as that is possible) is to climb a high mountain: you look out over all the other mountains, and after that it is a simple matter to find your way back to them and become better acquainted with them. But it is harder to orient the climber who is approaching Kant and his works. We try to find the simplest statements, to limit the essential operations to the decisive steps: we attempt succinct formulations that will quickly kindle the reader's thinking. Often as we may fail, we are bound to succeed in the end. For the deepest philosophical thoughts *must* be communicable. They can have true life only if people take possession of them.

But those who wish to understand must have patience. They must learn to recognize a thought in many different forms. Sooner or later, a light will dawn. We are not dealing with a mathematical idea, which can be captured by complicated operations, but with a revolution in thinking itself. We are not trying to grasp something as an object, but to carry out an objectless movement in the objective world. Of course it is necessary to learn a philosophical language, to grasp certain particular concepts. But all this has meaning only if one day the jolt occurs: the jolt of an insight, which is not mystical, not moral; not a revealed truth, but one which, in rational thinking, by thinking, transcends thinking itself.

Many attempts have been made to explain Kant. Of course we can say that the work is intelligible in itself, that the source excels every interpretation. This remains true (even if we hasten to add that a philosophy of this kind can reach a wide public only by way of interpretive expositions). Yet Kant himself expected others to develop the "path" he had cleared into a "broad highway." But there are two kinds of Kantians: those who settle forever in the framework of his categories, and those who, after reflecting, continue on the way with Kant.

Kant is the absolutely indispensable philosopher. Without him we have no basis for criticism in philosophy. But he is by no means the whole of philosophy. Working without images or concrete intuition, he opens up vast realms. But he does not fill them. With the forms he discovered, he made an immense contribution to the self-understanding of man; but he himself remains disembodied, because what he was, and what he was able to say, lie beyond any mere embodiment.

BIBLIOGRAPHY

EDITOR'S NOTE

The Bibliography is based on that given in the German original. English translations are given wherever possible. Selected English and American works have been added; these are marked by an asterisk.

SOURCES:

Sämtliche Werke, ed. by Karl Vorländer *et al.* (Philosophische Bibliothek.) 10 vols. Leipzig, Dürr, 1870-1905.

Gesammelte Schriften, ed. by Preussische Akademie der Wissenschaften. 22 vols. Berlin, Georg Reimer & Walter de Gruyter & Co., 1902-38. Includes letters and literary remains.

Die philosophischen Hauptvorlesungen Immanuel Kants, ed. by Arnold Kowalewski. Munich-Berlin, Gebr. Paetel, 1924.

Vorlesungen über die Metaphysik, ed. by K. H. Schmidt. Charlottenburg, Die Bücherwarte, 1924.

Eine Vorlesung Kants über Ethik, ed. by Paul Menzer. Berlin-Charlottenburg, Pan-Verlag, R. Heisl, 1924.

Vorlesungen über die philosophische Religionslehre, ed. by K. H. L. Pölitz. 2d ed. Leipzig, Taubert, 1830.

Reflexionen Kants zur kritischen Philosophie, ed. by Benno Erdmann. 2 vols. Leipzig, Fues, 1882-84.

Kants Leben in Darstellungen von Zeitgenossen, ed. by F. Gross, together with the biographies by Ludwig Ernst Borowski, Reinhold Bernhard Jachmann, and Ehregott Andreas Christian Wasianski. Berlin, Deutsches Bibliothek, 1912.

Johann Gottfried Hasse's Schrift: Letzte Äusserungen Kants und persönliche Notizen aus dem Opus Postumum, ed. by Artur Buchenau and Gerhard Lehmann. Berlin, W. de Gruyter & Co., 1925.

WORKS IN ENGLISH TRANSLATION, IN CHRONOLOGICAL ORDER:

Kant's Inaugural Dissertation and Early Writings on Space, trans. by John Handyside. Chicago, The Open Court, 1929.

Introduction to Logic and Essay on The Mistaken Subtlety of the Four Figures, trans. by Thomas Kingsmill Abbott. London, Longmans, 1885.

Dreams of a Visionary, Illustrated by Dreams of Metaphysics, by Emmanuel F. Goerwitz. New York, Macmillan, 1900.

Critique of Pure Reason, trans. by Norman Kemp Smith. New York, Humanities Press, 1950. (Abridged edition: New York, Modern Library, 1958.)

Prolegomena to Any Future Metaphysics, trans. by Lewis White Beck. New York, Liberal Arts Press, 1950.

Prolegomena to Any Future Metaphysics that Will Be Able to Present Itself as a Science, trans. by Peter G. Lucas. Manchester, Manchester University Press, 1953.

The Idea of a Universal History on a Cosmo-political Plan, trans. by Thomas De Quincy. Hanover, N. H., Sociological Press, 1927.

Fundamental Principles of the Metaphysic of Morals, trans. by Thomas Kingsmill Abbott. London, Longmans, 1895.

The Moral Law, or, Kant's Groundwork of the Metaphysic of Morals, trans. by Herbert James Paton. London, Hutchinson, 1948.

The Metaphysic of Ethics, trans. by J. W. Semple. 3d ed. Edinburgh, Clark, 1871.

Critique of Practical Reason and Other Works on the Theory of Ethics, trans. by Thomas Kingsmill Abbott. 6th ed., reissue. London, Longmans, 1948. (Also contains "Religion within the Bounds of Reason Only" and "On a Supposed Right to Lie out of Charity.")

Critique of Practical Reason, and Other Writings in Moral Philosophy, trans. by Lewis White Beck. Chicago, University of Chicago Press, 1949.

The Critique of Judgment, trans. by J. C. Meredith. New York, Oxford University Press, 1952.

The Critique of Judgment, trans. by John Henry Bernard. (Hafner Library of Classics Series.) New York, Hafner Pub. Co., 1951.

Eternal Peace, in *The Philosophy of Kant,* trans. and ed. by Carl Joachim Friedrich. New York, Modern Library, 1949.

Lectures on Ethics, trans. by Louis Infield of text published by Paul Menzer in 1924. New York, Century; London, Methuen, 1931. (Students' notes on Kant's lectures.)

COMMENTARIES:

To *Critique of Pure Reason:*

   *Cassirer, Heinrich Walter: *Kant's First Critique: an Appraisal of the Permanent Significance of Kant's Critique of Pure Reason.* London, G. Allen, 1955.

   *Paton, Herbert James: *Kant's Metaphysic of Experience: a Commentary on the First Half of the Kritik der reinen Vernunft.* 2 vols. London, Macmillan, 1936.

   *Smith, Norman Kemp: *A Commentary to Kant's Critique of Pure Reason.* 2d ed., rev. and enl. London, Macmillan, 1929.

   *Weldon, Thomas Dewar: *Introduction to Kant's Critique of Pure Reason.* Oxford, Clarendon Press, 1945.

To *Critique of Practical Reason:*

   *Paton, Herbert James: *The Categorical Imperative: a Study in Kant's Moral Philosophy.* London, Hutchinson, 1947.

To *Critique of Judgment:*

   *Cassirer, Heinrich Walter: *Commentary on Kant's Critique of Judgment.* London and Philadelphia, Methuen and W. B. Saunders, 1938.

SELECTED WORKS IN ENGLISH TRANSLATION:

The Living Thoughts of Kant, presented by Julien Benda. New York, McKay, 1940.

The Philosophy of Kant: Moral and Political Writings, ed. and trans. by Carl Joachim Friedrich. New York, Modern Library, 1949.

An Immanuel Kant Reader, trans. with commentary by Raymond Bernard Blakney. New York, Harper, 1960.

SECONDARY WORKS:

Bohatec, Josef: *Die Religionsphilosophie Kants in der "Religion innerhalb der Grenzen der blossen Vernunft," mit besonderer Berücksichtigung ihrer theologisch-dogmatischen Quellen.* Hamburg, Hoffmann & Campe, 1938.

Cassirer, Ernst: *Kants Leben und Lehre*. Berlin, Cassirer, 1918.

*Cohen, Morris Raphael: *Reason and Nature: an Essay on the Meaning of Scientific Method*. New York, Harcourt, Brace; London, Routledge, 1931.

Eisler, Rudolf: *Kant-Lexikon*. Berlin, E. S. Mittler & Sohn and Pan-Verlag Kurt Metzner, 1930.

*Friedrich, Carl Joachim: *Inevitable Peace*. Cambridge, Harvard University Press, 1948.

Hamann, Johann Georg: *Werke*. 1949.

Jaspers, Karl: "Das radikale Böse bei Kant," in *Rechenschaft und Ausblick*. Munich, Piper, 1951.

*Jones, William Thomas: *Morality and Freedom in the Philosophy of Immanuel Kant*. New York, Oxford University Press, 1940.

*Koerner, Stephan: *Kant*. Harmondsworth and Baltimore, Penguin Books, 1955.

Laas, Ernst: *Kants Stellung in der Geschichte des Conflikts zwischen Glauben und Wissen*. Berlin, Weidmann, 1882.

Lange, Frederick Albert: *The History of Materialism and Criticism of Its Present Importance*, trans. by Ernest Chester Thomas. 3 vols. in 1. 3d ed. New York, Harcourt, Brace; London, Kegan Paul, 1925.

*Lindsay, Alexander Dunlop: *Kant*. New York and London, Peter Smith and Oxford University Press, 1934.

*Macmillan, Robert Alexander Cameron: *The Crowning Phase of Critical Philosophy: a Study in Kant's Critique of Judgment*. New York, Macmillan, 1912.

Paulsen, Friedrich: *Immanuel Kant, His Life and Doctrine*, trans. from rev. German ed. by J. E. Creighton and Albert Lefevre. New York, Scribner, 1902.

Reich, Klaus: *Die Vollständigkeit der Kantischen Urteilstafel*. 2d ed. Berlin, R. Schoetz, 1948.

Rosenkranz, Karl: *Geschichte der Kant'schen Philosophie*. Leipzig, Voss, 1840.

Scheler, Max: *Der Formalismus in der Ethik und die materiale Wertethik*. 4th ed. Berne, Francke Verlag, 1954.

Stavenhagen, Kurt: *Kant und Königsberg*. Göttingen, Deuerlich, 1949.

Troeltsch, Ernst: *Das Historische in Kants Religionsphilosophie: Zugleich ein Beitrag zu den Untersuchungen über Kants Philosophie der Geschichte*. Berlin, Reuther & Reichard, 1904.

Vaihinger, Hans: *Kommentar zu Kants Kritik der reinen Vernunft*. 2 vols. 2d ed. Stuttgart-Berlin-Leipzig, Union, 1922.

Vorländer, Karl: *Immanuel Kant: der Mann und das Werk*. 2 vols. Leipzig, F Meiner, 1924.

INDEX OF NAMES

Books by Karl Jaspers
available in paperback editions
from Harcourt Brace Jovanovich, Inc.

THE GREAT PHILOSOPHERS

VOLUME I

SOCRATES, BUDDHA, CONFUCIUS, JESUS

PLATO AND AUGUSTINE

KANT

THE GREAT PHILOSOPHERS

VOLUME II

ANAXIMANDER, HERACLITUS, PARMENIDES,
PLOTINUS, LAO-TZU, NAGARJUNA

ANSELM AND NICHOLAS OF CUSA

SPINOZA